MIDDLESBROUGH FC
THE UNSEEN HISTORY

MIDDLESBROUGH FC
THE UNSEEN HISTORY

Richard Piers Rayner

breedon **books**
PUBLISHING

First published in Great Britain in 2008 by
The Breedon Books Publishing Company Limited
Breedon House, 3 The Parker Centre,
Derby, DE21 4SZ.

ISBN: 978-1-85983-639-2

Printed and bound by Scotprint, Haddington, Scotland.

CONTENTS

Introduction

This is not a conventional history and not all of that which follows might be exactly as it happened. But where I have fictionalised certain situations I believe that this book remains as true as it is possible to be to the spirit of events that occurred in some instances over a hundred years ago. All the dates and all the games detailed are true and if I have put words into the mouths of people who are themselves long gone, I believe they are the words they would have spoken had they been presented with the opportunity to do so. I have tried to recreate the world in which they lived and loved and played the game and for a brief while at least bring them all back to life again. Thanks are due, in no small measure and for a variety of reasons, including research on Middlesbrough and other clubs, all round helpfulness, information and general support, to Peter Buckman, Tony Byles, Mike Church, Andrew Dennis, Colin Foster, Nigel Gibb, Harry Glasper, Michelle Grainger and everyone at Breedon Books, Michael Joyce, David Moor, Joe Nolan, Stuart Pacitto at Teesside Archives, Peter N and Jean M Rayner, Michael J Rayner, and Lisa Whadcock. Very special mention is due for Dave Allan, Graham Bell, Liz Allison at MFC and indeed all the staff and players of the club, past, present and future. And the biggest thank you of all is to Bernadette Ann Nolan, my beloved partner and co-creator (you can blame her for the Tripe Supper joke).

Richard P Rayner, July 2008.

Chapter One
Sherlock Holmes
and the Fratton Park Mystery

It is impossible to tell the story of any single football club without coming to the realisation that it is all part of a much bigger picture. So, while this is the story of Middlesbrough Football Club, it is also part of the story of every other club that has crossed their path; every club that was formed in the mists of a forgotten Victorian winter to take a clattering muddy booted step into the present day.

You have to start somewhere, and where better to begin than with a typical mystery? An example of the sort of story that the sporting world of the mid to late 19th century has in such rich abundance. Goodness knows, there are mysteries enough to tax the ingenuity of even the greatest detective.

'So, Watson, what do you make of our little mystery?' asked Sherlock Holmes.

He had been watching with a slightly amused glint in his eye as I pored through my extensive collection of *Rothmans Football Yearbooks*.

'I must admit,' I said, 'that I have given the matter a great deal of thought.'

'Excellent!' he exclaimed. 'Then please keep me in suspense no longer. Tell me all, remembering to omit no detail, however slight.'

'Well, Holmes, it seems perfectly clear to me that this fellow A.C. Smith, who was a founder and original playing member of Portsmouth AFC from 1884 to 1890, was none other than our own esteemed creator, Mister Arthur Conan Doyle. And therefore I have no hesitation in proclaiming that he was indeed the first goalkeeper, and occasional right-back, for the Fratton Park club.'

Sherlock Holmes.

'As ever, Watson, you come to your conclusions quickly,' proclaimed Holmes. 'And, if I may say so, you state them with admirable clarity…'

I started to blush immodestly, before He added:

'Of course, they are also completely wrong.'

Resisting the impulse to throw one of my heavier volumes at him, I asked Holmes to explain himself.

'As you know Watson, our own first published adventure appeared in *Beeton's Christmas Annual* in 1887.'

'Yes, obviously,' I replied, somewhat tersely. 'In the story, *A Study in Scarlet*. Everyone knows that.'

The mysterious Mister Smith.

'As you say. And, at this time, as you yourself have observed, Mister Conan Doyle, a resident of Southsea, was plying his talents between the sticks at Portsmouth AFC. Would you just remind me of the year?'

'Really, Holmes, I wish you wouldn't take me for quite such a fool. It was 1887.'

'I'm obliged to you. Then, I wonder if you would mind explaining how the gentleman could claim any involvement with the modern-day club that was not, in fact, founded until 1898? At which time, enjoying the fruits of our own best-selling success, Conan Doyle had moved on to Vienna, London, the Americas...'

'So it's safe to assume he could not have been in Portsmouth during the year in question?'

Frank Brettell.

'Exactly, Watson. You hit the nail on the head precisely! Portsmouth FC evolved not from the amateur team Portsmouth AFC, who may well claim the distinction of being the first club in the town, but from a different amateur side, the Royal Artillery Club. Retaining, by the way, the services of their goalkeeper, Matt Reilly, as their first official custodian.'

He paused to light his pipe, filling the room with a noxious cloud of tobacco smoke, before continuing:

'The credit for the success of Portsmouth as a professional football club should belong to their secretary manager, a Mister Frank Brettell, who had previously done similar work for Tottenham Hotspur and Bolton Wanderers. He had also been a player for Everton and a reporter for the *Liverpool Mercury*.'

'You're a wonder Holmes,' I was agog with admiration. 'I don't know how you do it.'

'It's elementary, my dear fellow,' he sighed. 'Really, it's quite elementary.'

Chapter Two

The Clatter of Boots

In 1892, Richard Daft, the famous Nottinghamshire cricketer, known as the W.G. Grace of the north, was talking about the earliest days of professional football in the area:

'I played centre-forward, but I'm not sure about this as we were never very particular in those days of keeping one's place. Charging and dribbling were the chief features of the game at that time.'

Richard Daft.

No one regarded it as the least bit odd if the teams set out in a typical formation of nine forwards and two backs, and a fairly relaxed view was taken of the number of on-field participants per team. For instance, Middlesbrough FC's first-ever training session in the spring of 1876 had approximately 35 players on each side, though this was gradually whittled away as the hardier types prevailed and went on to form the basis of the first Boro team. The Football Association was founded in 1863, and only Blackheath withdrew, regarding the new rule that banned the hacking of shins as new-wave nonsense that would ruin the modern game. Tripping and elbowing were also perfectly legal tactics, as was charging the goalkeeper, whether he had the ball in his possession or not. It is entirely possible that, a few years later, it was the sort of ensuing scrimmage in the latter circumstance that would convince Jeremiah Dawkings, the Middlesbrough 'keeper, that it might be a good idea to not continue smoking his pipe during games. Presumably he only did it if play was at the other end.

Among the remaining 11 sides in 1863 was Notts County, founded a year earlier, at the time of the American Civil War, and the oldest surviving professional football team in the world.

They had been a gentlemen's only club and played at the Hollow in the Park, in the grounds of Nottingham Castle, before moving to Trent Bridge Cricket Ground in 1883 and then Meadow Lane in 1910.

Out of the confusion of the early days, County emerged as eventual FA Cup winners on 31 March 1894, beating Bolton Wanderers 4–1 at Goodison Park. Richard Daft

would probably take particular pride in his youngest son, Harry Butler Daft, whom he had played cricket with in the county XI at Kennington Oval against Surrey in 1891, sitting on the far right in the picture of the Cup-winning team (on page 12). Exemplifying the relaxed attitude towards how many teams a popular player could turn out for at one time, Harry was also a member of the Corinthians club, put in the occasional appearance for Nottingham Forest and could usually get a game with Newark too, if he happened to have brought his boots along with him.

One place removed from Harry Daft in the County team picture, on the same row, is poor doomed Jimmy Logan. He scored a hat-trick in the Final, and only Townsley of Blackburn in 1890 and Mortensen of Blackpool in 1953 could ever say the same, but it was a brief moment of glory. Two years later, he was a player with Loughborough at an away game with Newton Heath. Unfortunately, his team made a fundamental error before they even set foot on the pitch. They forgot to bring their kit with them. But men were made of stern stuff in those days, and they just had to roll their sleeves up and get on with it – quite literally. The Loughborough team played the game in the clothes they were standing up in. And it rained, and it rained, and it rained. Soaked to the skin and then some,

Notts County were founded during the period of the American Civil War.

The Notts County team.
The County Cup Final team line up:
Back: Charlie Bramley, Theophilus Harper, David Calderhead, George Toone, Jack Hendry, Alf Shelton, Joe Goode (trainer).
Front: Arthur Watson, Sam Donnelly, Jimmy Logan, Dan Bruce, Harry Daft.

they had to endure the train journey home, during which time Jimmy Logan caught a chill. A few days later it turned into pneumonia, and he never recovered. He was only 25 when he died.

Notts County had quite an influence on the developing game. In the same year as winning the Cup Final, they finished third from top of Division Two and played Preston, who had finished third from bottom of Division One, in a 'Test Match', the format for which was similar to the initial concept of the end-of-season Play-offs in the modern game. The winner would be the team to play at the top level in the next season, and Preston duly preserved their top-flight status with a 4–0 victory.

County were also instrumental in the introduction of penalty-kicks in 1891, after an FA Cup tie against Stoke when the Notts back, Hendry, fisted the goalbound ball clear. Stoke failed to benefit from the awarded free-kick. They can also claim a significant influence in world football. In 1905 Juventus Football Club of Turin, in the Italian League, were getting a bit disillusioned with their pink polka-dotted shirts. The cheap material had faded over the years, and they were on the lookout for something a bit more distinctive (or, possibly, less pink). Enter their player John Savage, originally of Nottingham, who provided a set of County's black-and-white-striped shirts for the use of a club that would become one of the great European club sides.

Not that County could afford to be at all sniffy about pink polka-dotted shirts. They had not been beyond experimenting with different styles themselves. In the 1800s they had had brief flirtations with black-and-amber hoops, chocolate-and-blue halves, before going along with Juventus in agreeing that the black-and-white-striped look was the way they wanted history to remember them.

That was all typical then of the sporting world, if not the changing face of the world itself, in the 19th century. But this is the story of one club, and while, in 1894, Notts County were winning the FA Cup and Arthur Conan Doyle's Portsmouth amateurs were disbanding, Tom Bach was leading the charge as Middlesbrough Association Football Club won their first Northern League title and, on the day of the FA Cup Final, were beating Darlington 2–0 at Stockton, winning the Cleveland Senior Cup to add to their impressive collection of Victorian-age silverware.

Tom Bach leading the charge.

In 1886 Boro beat Redcar 8–1 to win the Cleveland Cup Final in front of 7,000 spectators.

There is a myth that, apart from a comparatively recent success in Cardiff, Middlesbrough FC and Cup Final victories are strangers to each other. History, however, tells a different story. As long ago as 1882, the Boro beat Redcar 2–1 to win the Cleveland Cup, retaining the trophy over the next four years, beating the same opposition on each occasion. They had also, somewhat less successfully, been playing in the FA Cup since 1883.

Redcar (again) knocked them out in January 1886, but they got their comeuppance in the Cleveland Cup Final in April when Boro maintained their grip on the old trophy with a resounding 8–1 victory in front of 7,000 spectators. True to the Corinthian Sporting Spirit, Middlesbrough withdrew from the next season's competition in order 'to give the others a chance.' This admirable resolve only lasted a year, however, and in 1888 normal service was resumed with a 3–0 Final victory over Stockton. The next year Redcar beat them in the semi-final, but it was at a time when the Boro were moving on and were only months away from their first Northern League season and in the meantime, by way of compensation, won the Cleveland Senior Cup against Stockton. Although they lost out on that Cup the next year, they regained it in the aforementioned Final in 1894.

But that was not the beginning of the story.

Charging was a perfectly legal tactic.

Chapter Three

The Legend of the Tripe Supper

While Alexander Graham Bell was inventing the telephone, Fred Hardisty had an even better idea.

In 1876 there was a man who, sick to death of not being able to find out the latest football scores, set out to do something about it. Fortunately, for himself and for the rest of the world, his name was Alexander Graham Bell and he was able to alleviate that unfortunate situation by inventing the telephone.

On 20 October of that same year Fred Hardisty of Middlesbrough, who no doubt thought that Mister Bell might be onto something with his excellent idea, had a groundbreaking venture of his own that he was about to undertake. This no doubt occupied his thoughts as he took the tram (horse-drawn, it was still a good 20 years before electrification) along Linthorpe Road to his meeting with the other cricket club members and Frederick Thompson, the chap from the south who had recently arrived in town with rather an intriguing notion.

The meeting took place in the gymnasium behind the Albert Park Hotel, and Mister Thompson's idea was for the formation of an Association Football Club. He had played the game himself in the south, where its popularity was growing, and even earned himself something of a reputation, if they did not mind him mentioning it, and if there was a better way for cricketers to keep fit during the winter then he would like to know what it was.

Fred Hardisty could not have agreed more. Along with Jackson Ewbank and Charles Booth, he was happy to go along with the idea of having a further meeting that would formalise the arrangement. And why not have a bite of dinner at the same time? He knew just the place.

So, in November of 1876, in the Talbot Hotel, on the corner of South Street opposite to the Town Hall and market place in Middlesbrough, they reconvened to create their own little piece of history.

The tram from Linthorpe Village.

The Talbot Hotel on the far right-hand side of South Street, where history was made.

Legend has it that as these worthy gentlemen went about their task they tucked into a tripe supper, and it may well be the case. But, at the same time, it must be acknowledged that they were all ex-public schoolboys and may possibly have had slightly more sophisticated palates. Poor Frederick Thompson, fresh from the luxury of southern dining tables, would have been more than a little taken aback by the white and wobbly tripe that may have been presented to him for his supper. For instance, a typical middle-class dinner at the time would consist of soup, fish, roast beef, stewed apples, jelly and fruit, with plenty of time between courses for the imbibing of fortifying fluids. And that was doubtless what Frederick would have been expecting. Fred Hardisty, too, was an accountant of some repute who would become chairman of the newly formed club and was used to more sophisticated fare, but it is worth conjuring up an image of them gathered round the table. Jackson Ewbank is on the left, next to Frederick Thompson, with Fred Hardisty on the right.

He is responding to the waiter who has just asked him, 'How do you like your tripe, sir?' Anticipating years of suffering on the terraces, Mister Hardisty replies, 'Preferably not served up on Saturday afternoons.'

Waiter: 'How do you like your tripe, sir?' *Hardisty:* 'Preferably not served up on Saturday afternoons.'

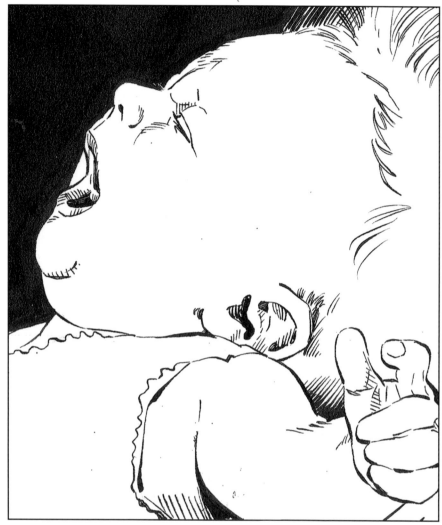

Bob Wanless makes his entrance into the world.

That is the thing with legends of course. You can never be quite sure what to believe. But one thing is certain, whatever they did or did not have sloshing about in their insides as they came out of the Talbot Hotel into the lantern light of South Street, with an icy mist drifting in off the Tees, they had founded Middlesbrough Football Club.

On 19 July 1876 an event had occurred in Middlesbrough, which was apparently irrelevant to the great enterprise of Messrs Ewbank, Thompson, Hardisty and Booth et al, but of inestimable importance to the Wanless family of the town.

They, or to be more precise Mrs Wanless in particular, had given birth to a baby boy. He was christened 'Robert', and more than anyone else young Robert would provide a link from the gaslit world where it all began to the new age of a modern-day football club. We will hear his name again.

Chapter Four

Thirty Five-a-side

The Christmas time of 1876 was freezing cold. Snow drifted across the fields that bordered Middlesbrough, and the breath steamed from the horses that drew the trams back and forth between the town in the north and Linthorpe Village in the south. But Fred Hardisty was on his way home after a long day of accountancy, and that was cause enough for quiet satisfaction. It could take an age in the unheated carriage but, if he could first clear the frosty window glass, he had the compensation of glimpsing the occasional villa, only partially obscured by winter dark trees, where there was always a warm festive glow. 'God Bless Her Majesty', he very probably thought, and 'God bless her consort Prince Albert' too. It was thanks to that ennobled gentleman that three decades earlier people had started to decorate and illuminate Christmas trees in their living rooms, a fashion the Prince had inspired from his home in the Duchy of Saxony and which was really starting to catch on. They had become an inestimably cheerful sight.

As the tram continued its slow progress, Mister Hardisty could take in what he could see of the sights. On his left just past the junction with Southfield Road was the old cricket ground, or, to give it its full name, the Swatter's Carr Linthorpe Road East Cricket Ground. It still seemed like yesterday that the old ground had hosted not just first-class cricket, with a Yorkshire versus Lancashire game as recently as 1867, but it had been Middlesbrough Cricket Club's home too. It was where for the past 20 years, every summer, victories had been fought for, draws tolerated and defeats endured. It was not just cricket either – over the years the site had hosted an annual fair, and sometimes there had been other ball games. There was even an unofficial kickabout or two that predated the formalised rules of Association Football. The rumour now was that the field was up for sale. They said they were going to build an Opera House on the site. Well, Mister Hardisty supposed, change was inevitable. Behind that fence they were passing on his right was the new cricket field, all in darkness now, where the club had moved to. Next to it was the rugby field where Tees Wanderers played their games.

Mister Hardisty's friend Oswald 'Ossie' Cochrane, Oxford graduate, local solicitor and town coroner, was one of their players and had expressed enthusiastic interest in the newly formed Association Football Club, to the extent that he was certain he could help the new sporting venture get off the ground. Perhaps he might be able to arrange a fixture or two and, as an all-round sportsman himself, if there was an opening in the team he had an idea, as something of an amateur boxer too, that the role of centre-half might be right up his street. Mister Hardisty thought it all looked very promising. He pulled his collar up as his breath clouded the window glass again. Turning the other way, he looked across the carriage and glimpsed the distant faint lights of Park Villas not quite obscured by the shadowy wind-blown trees inbetween. That meant another point of interest was coming up next. And there it was. Albert Park. Named after the aforementioned Prince Consort, where just a week or so ago Mister Hardisty, whether he realised it or not (and, to be fair, most likely he did not), along with his fellow sporting enthusiasts had delivered to the town an early Christmas present of unsurpassable value. Their very first organised game of football.

Mister Hardisty travelled onwards, passing again on his left-hand side the Albert Park Hotel, where it had all begun, towards his destination, that comfortable home of his in Linthorpe. But, much as the warmth of the fireside was an undeniable enticement, there was a part of him that remained and strayed across the frost-bound fields beyond the trees to relive the moment. His first loyalty, just the same as everybody else, had been to the cricket field. Not that there was any guarantee how many people would respond to the announcement of an inaugural practice match for Middlesbrough Football Club, even a handful of athletic young men chasing a ball about a winter-blighted greensward were bound to do damage to the sodden ground. So using their own field, or even the rugby-dedicated field next door, was out of the question even if the owners, representatives of Middlesbrough Estate, would have permitted it, or perhaps more pertinently if the footballers would have been prepared to meet the cost of renting the ground. Nevertheless, the question still remained: where would the game be played? Albert Park was the natural choice. The fellows had already indulged in the occasional kick-about, just to get the hang of things, on the Archery Ground that was part of those hallowed environs, and there was plenty of open ground all around. Just so long as the park commissioners could be persuaded that it was a good idea.

They may well have had their misgivings, but the would-be footballers were men with accomplished persuasive powers. Among them were those who had persuaded a High Court Judge or two to either don or not the dreaded black cap, and before such intellects the park commissioners, if not exactly wilting, certainly gave way, and pointed out that the park's own cricket field was available at a very reasonable rate.

'That'll do nicely,' chorused all interested parties.

One hundred and thirteen years before Kevin Costner was told, 'If you build it, they will come,' in the motion picture *Field of Dreams*, a film about baseball but relevant nonetheless, the gentlemen of Middlesbrough Cricket Club and the newly formed Middlesbrough Football Club might well have taken similar advice: 'If you go to the park, they will follow.'

Because that is just what had happened.

It had hardly been a masterpiece of organisation. For a start there were no changing room facilities, and the participants had donned their various different strips at home before making their way to the park. And as they did so, they were joined along the way by curious onlookers who wanted to find out what was going on. There was no matching uniformity in what the players wore. It was a question of digging out the old school colours and making the best of it. Other interested parties turned up to try their luck in the clothes they stood up in, coats buttoned up against the cold. Some were there just out of curiosity and because there were limited opportunities for healthy diversions on a Victorian winter afternoon. They came to watch the ongoing drama, but there were others who were determined to join in, to try their luck out on the field. After all, how hard could it be to kick a ball between two wooden posts?

Frederick Thompson dribbled 'in the speedy public school fashion around the novices.'

By kick-off time quite a throng had gathered and something like 35 players or more on each side prepared to do battle in front of a steadily growing audience. The parks committee had expressed their doubts and the cricket ground that formed almost the entire field of play might not recover until well into the summer, but there was no time for regrets or for looking back. With a dull thud, the first boot touched the heavy leather football, and the game was underway.

And, of course, it was not as easy as it looked. After half an hour or so, a lot of the novices had dropped out and joined the crowd on the touchline as the serious athletes got down to business. By the time that the fading light had brought things to a halt Fred Hardisty, Jackson Ewbank, Charles Booth, Ossie Cochrane and those others that remained standing, breathless, mud covered but triumphant as the evening gloom settled around the park, had created the nucleus of a team. Now all that remained was to find someone to play against.

As they left the park by the main gate, open fields lay before them. This area between Middlesbrough and Linthorpe had an odd sounding name. Hardly surprising when you realise it was derived from the Old Norse name Iarhusum, 'the Little Houses by the River.' It had been a settlement on the banks of the Tees where Viking longboats had once lain at anchor. For some reason, and while no one present could quite put his finger on why it should be the case, the name was eerily significant. Evolving variously through the ages from Arsum to Aersum, it had eventually become known by its present form: Ayresome. The Vikings were long gone of course, and now the only signs of life were the twinkling lights of Oldgate Farm, closer at hand than the duller illumination of the St Barnabas Church Mission away in the distance not far from the site where there were plans underway to build a Union Workhouse. Further away, at the edge of the fields, was a flooded piece of land where a low mist hung over the dark water.

Oldgate. They had the Scandinavians to thank for that too. Where they were standing outside the main park gates had once been part of what the Danes had called the Old Gat, or Old Road, and beyond the farm long ago would have been the crossroads, where a dissecting road made its way southwards across the lower ground that was then under the floodwater. The Hollow Road or, as any Viking could have told you, the Hol Gat. Another name that would have resonance in the years to come.

Trudging homeward, perhaps squelching slightly, Ossie Cochrane had made his proposition, somewhat breathlessly after his afternoon exertions, to Fred Hardisty and the others. There were only three other teams in the North East at that time: South Bank and Barnard Castle and Tyne Club in Newcastle. An old school friend of Ossie Cochrane had formed the latter team, and he was certain he would be able to arrange a game. In addition,

The team coach.
First man on the right: 'Come on, Boro.'
Second man: 'Hey, that's quite catchy.'

Mister Cochrane was quite certain that the rugby team he represented, Tees Wanderers, would be interested in having a go at the new Association game and could be relied upon to provide spirited opposition.

'Welcome aboard, Mister Cochrane,' Fred Hardisty had said, or something very like it. 'Centre-half, you say? Yes, I think that can be arranged.'

'Of course, you realise that the Park Committee is never going to allow us to use the cricket field again,' someone else then pointed out. 'I mean, did you see the state we left it in?'

'Good point,' agreed Mister Hardisty. 'We're going to have to find a more permanent home. But the park is such a convenient location.'

'Well, you know…there's always the Archery Ground.'

Ossie Cochrane

Ossie Cochrane, was as good as, if not better than, his word. He wasted no time in getting down to organising Middlesbrough Football Club's inaugural fixture list in 1877. Tees Wanderers and Tyne Club, in all honesty there were not many other options, were duly pencilled in, and there remained only the question of transportation.

Ossie Cochrane.

Fortunately, they did not have to travel far. Tees Wanderers played their games on the rugby ground next to the cricket pitch further along Linthorpe Road towards the town, which was well within walking distance for everybody concerned, and if a meeting with Tyne Club in Newcastle presented something of a sterner challenge then Mister Cochrane was equal to it.

The team coach may not have exactly been luxurious and might have given the bones a bit of a shaking, but it did the job as well as could be expected, and it was surprising what could be endured with a rug snugly tucked around you and something to warm the cockles for each man's hip flask.

Ossie Cochrane was only 20 years old in 1877, but he would still be playing in 1889, by which time he would have captained the Boro to three Cleveland Cup successes and played in two more. All of this while finding time to get himself elected as chairman of the club, joining his old friend Fred Hardisty (who would also serve as a non-playing chairman until 1892) on the board. He was a firm believer in the nobility of the amateur game, totally in accordance with Vivian Woodward, the great centre-forward of Tottenham, Chelsea and England, who would not even accept the remuneration of his bus fare to matches.

Mister Cochrane had the casting vote that retained the Boro's amateur status in 1886 when the new wave of professionalism was becoming a force that was increasingly hard to disregard and which was already the cause of dissention in the ranks – in fact there was some real trouble brewing. But the event that would change the club forever was still three years away. By that time, Ossie Cochrane would have represented the Boro in the Cleveland Cup and the FA Cup and countless friendly games that comprised the club's earliest fixtures until they joined the newly formed Northern League in 1889.

And he did indeed become Middlesbrough Football Club's first centre-half.

Chapter Five
No Place Like Home:
The Archery Ground

Whatever the results were of those two initial games, away to the Tyne Club and then Tees Wanderers, they are lost in the bleak midwinter of late 1876 and early 1877. That is if anyone even bothered to keep count. But the return fixture with the Wanderers is a different story.

By the time it came around on 24 February 1877, arrangements had been made with the Commissioners of Albert Park to use the archery field on the northern edge of the park. Though it is entirely possible that the Park Committee people wished they had thought to hide behind their desks when the footballing fellows came knocking on their door again, they could hardly turn down their latest application. Not that there was even the slightest chance that they would let them use the cricket field again, but the archery field? Well, that was a slightly different proposition. After all, the Middlesbrough lacrosse and baseball teams both used the ground (though not the archery club, oddly), so it was hardly fair to say no to a further sporting venture. What harm could it do? And so, the Old Archery Ground in Albert Park became Middlesbrough Football Club's first home.

Jackson Ewbank.

The first proper game to be played there was the return fixture against Tees Wanderers, and Jackson Ewbank was about to make a name for himself; because this time the media would be in attendance. Or, at least, reporters from the *North Eastern Daily Gazette* and the *Weekly Exchange* no less, were there, pencils poised at the ready and notebooks in hand.

The multitude of colours that had dazzled the local populace in the earlier practice games was no longer on show. All the shirts had been dyed a uniform dark blue, and this time they looked like a proper team, though the representatives of the Parks Committee may have groaned inwardly to see so many spectators turning up to trample the turf. And worse was to come.

As one of the park keepers remarked to his friend: 'That fellow over there, the one with the spade. What on earth is he doing?'

'He's digging holes,' explained his friend. 'They say they need somewhere to stick their goalposts.'

The park keeper had an idea where he would like to see the vandals stick their goalposts, but he was far too well brought up to express it. Still, there was no denying that there was significant local interest in the event. There must have been at least 100 people, if not more, who turned up to watch the game on a wild and blustery February day.

The wind caught the spray from the park's ornamental fountain as the crowd gathered and the match umpires, handkerchiefs in hand in case they had to signal that they had spotted an infringement, got the game underway. (Only a couple of years later a whistle would be used by the match official for the first time in a game between Nottingham Forest and Sheffield Norfolk.)

Midway through the first half the moment arrived. Jackson Ewbank broke away from a melee of players, and the world, or at least that part of it occupied by 100 or so Teessiders, held its breath because history was about to be made.

If Jackson Ewbank is now remembered for more than his admittedly admirable ability to grow an enormous moustache, it is down to that moment on 24 February 1877 when he prepared to boot the ball into the unguarded goal. It would be Middlesbrough Football Club's first recorded goal.

The man in the bowler hat, by the way, is not some prototypical hooligan interfering with proceedings, but one of the match umpires, who would normally be expected to remain on the periphery of the action, struggling to keep up with play. Which is not to say that, even in those distant times, hooliganism was not much of a problem. As early as 1885 it was being reported that players were attacked with stones and sticks after Preston North End beat Aston Villa 5–1. An outraged media described the offenders as 'howling roughs.' And my grandad told me of a similar incident when the Middlesbrough faithful, also armed with sticks, indulged themselves by chasing the visiting Arsenal team back down the tunnel just as they prepared to take to the field.

None of which should detract from Mister Ewbanks's moment of glory. And we may safely assume that the crowd that day were on their best behaviour, satisfying themselves by politely applauding the ensuing heroics as the game against Tees Wanderers ended 1–1 after a second-half equaliser for the visitors.

And, just in order to orientate ourselves as to where everything stood in relation to the modern world, in the background of the illustration (on page 30) showing Jackson Ewbank about to score his historic goal, Park Road North runs next to the Archery Field. The building on the left is Park Villas, and it still stands today, becoming part of Parkside Maternity Hospital in 1920, and is now engulfed by the university halls of residence. On the right, the twin-gabled house is standing

Jackson Ewbank prepares to break free of the pack, and history is about to be made…

on roughly the present-day site of Nazareth House. The original building was opened as a 'Catholic Orphanage and House for the Aged Poor' in 1884. But at the time of the Middlesbrough games on the Archery Ground it was a private residence. Nazareth House, as we would recognize it today, was built in 1905–06.

So the year passed and interest in football spread throughout the North East as more new clubs were established, although thankfully that rattletrap of a team coach that Middlesbrough used never had to travel too far to fulfil a fixture, since the majority of games were local affairs. And, since being frozen half to death and shaken until your bones felt like they had been forcibly disarranged and put back together in the wrong order were hardly the best preparations for playing a game of football, it was possibly the team coach we can blame for the Boro's first defeat, 1–0 away to those giants of the world game, Barnard Castle, on 22 December 1877.

...as he scores the Boro's first-ever recorded goal.

In the meantime, the Boro welcomed the likes of South Bank, Loftus, Eston and their old friends Tyne Club of Newcastle to the Archery Ground. There was still no organised competition as such, but more opportunities were arising to play friendly games against other enthusiasts, and when that was not possible even a game between the first team and the reserves would always attract a decent enough crowd. Attendances grew, and by the early part of 1878 as many as 200 people at a time were turning up to cheer the team on. Which may explain why Boro's stay at the Archery Ground was short-lived. As we have seen, the Park Commissioners had always been a little uneasy about the sporting endeavours of the footballers, and things had not improved as the game's popularity increased.

By 1879, more and more complaints were being made about the state of the ground due to football being played on it. Undoubtedly the Boro crowds trampling the turf had not helped. After numerous complaints, and having done as much damage as the old Archery Ground could stand, the club was given its marching orders. 'And you can take your goalposts with you!'

In March of 1879 Boro moved to Breckon Hill Road.

Breckon Hill Road

In reality, it was nothing more than a farmer's field (the farmer in question being a Mister Kemp) in what is now the Longlands area of Middlesbrough. The field lay roughly in the same area as Breckon Hill School playing fields would one day occupy.

Admission to games was threepence for men and a penny for boys, with ladies being admitted free. Your money was collected by a gentleman who came round with a white bowl, and the cheery clatter of coin as it clanged onto the enamel did not go unnoticed by Mister Kemp. When he looked into it he saw that matchday takings could sometimes be as high as £3 and, with his farmer's eye for a good deal, immediately suggested putting up the rent for the field. The club decided an even better idea would be if they moved on yet again.

The picture overleaf is from a game played in that single season at Breckon Hill. Jack Harrison (who played as a forward in the first Archery Ground game) is the goalkeeper dealing with that relatively recent innovation, the corner-kick (introduced in 1872), though up until 1912 as a 'keeper he would have been allowed to handle the ball anywhere on the field. Billy Pickstock is in the foreground, looking on.

The crossbar was another modern device, having replaced tape at some grounds in 1875 but only made obligatory later on, in 1882. Goal nets and penalty-kicks were still some years away from being introduced. Pickstock, who had made his Boro debut that season, went on to become a crowd favourite during the 1880s, despite refusing to head the ball and always wearing his cap.

The final match at Breckon Hill was a 3–0 win over Loftus on 7 February 1880. Jackson Ewbank, already in the history books and showing the kind of form that would lead to county honours (he had already become club captain, a post he held for six years), claimed all three strikes against Loftus. And another hero was about to make his debut too.

Action from Breckon
Hill Road.

Borrie of the Boro

On 3 April 1882 the outlaw Jesse James was shot in the back and killed in St Joseph, Missouri, by Robert Ford, and it is probable that as a consequence he never heard the news that a couple of days earlier Middlesbrough, having overcome Guisborough and North Ormesby along the way, had won the Cleveland Cup Final for the first time, beating Redcar 2–1 after a replay. Among the Boro team, though not the scorers, was the solicitor, Albert Borrie, who having signed for the club in 1879 was already on his way to becoming one of the great goal-getters of those early years. (And, indeed, goal-stopper too. He played at least one game as 'keeper in October 1887 in an FA Cup Qualifying tie against Hallam of Sheffield, keeping a clean sheet in a 6–0 victory.)

Boro had started playing Sheffield Cup games to augment the friendlies that comprised the greater part of their fixture list in the 1879–80 season and attracted (much to Mister Kemp's chagrin) 1,000 spectators to the Linthorpe Road Ground for a defeat against Sheffield Exchange in which Fred Hardisty, despite a heroic personal effort at the back, was starting to think that the physical side of the game was getting a bit much for him and that his skills might be better

Borrie of the Boro.

He never took his cap off, except to doff it politely, and he refused to head the ball, but Billy Pickstock became a crowd favourite.

employed at an administrative level. Then, in 1880 over 2,500 somehow squeezed into the ground to see a draw against Redcar. Boro won the replay 3–1 with another Ewbank hat-trick, but the spotlight was shifting and Albert Borrie was preparing to step into it.

After the Cleveland Association was established in 1881, the Cleveland Challenge Cup got going, and along with his teammates Albert Borrie rolled up his sleeves and was ready for action. He played in the five Cleveland Cup victories between 1882 and 1886, and if he missed out on scoring in the first one he made up for it by putting it between the sticks (goal nets were not introduced until 1891) in the subsequent Final, scoring twice in a 3–2 victory over Redcar again. He then failed to score in the 1884 Final before succeeding again twice in 1886. Albert also played in Middlesbrough's first FA Cup tie in 1883, on the losing side, this time to Staveley, before scoring in an historic first victory in the competition the next year against Newark. He retired from playing in 1889, just before the Boro set off on their Northern League adventure, but still served the club as secretary until 1895.

Chapter Six

The Road to Linthorpe

Goalkeeper in the pre-Northern League games, Jeremiah Dawkings, was seldom far removed from his pipe. Especially if play was at the other end.

Shortly before his death in 1955, a certain Mister Oswald Henry Cochrane was shown around Ayresome Park. Marvelling at the grand stadium, he looked up at the wide-open terraces of the East End of the ground and made a gesture with his stick.

'There used to be a farm right about there,' he said, pointing towards the boys enclosure. 'Oldgate Farm. Yes, that was it.'

Perhaps he remembered the lost days of his youth. Of standing with his friends muddy and soaked to the skin after that first practice match outside the main gates of Albert Park on a winter evening 79 years earlier, looking across the fields towards the distant lights of the farm in the distance. Was it really so long ago?

'And here,' he waved his stick in the general direction of the playing area, 'this was a very hollow ground, liable to flooding. In the winter it looked like there was a lake here.'

He paused, remembering days that had passed, before returning to the matter at hand:

'In our day we simply wanted to enjoy a game of football,' he said. 'But, you know, it all outgrew us.'

He could have made a comment or two about the rise of professionalism and of how it spoiled everything, but he refrained. The early 1900s had proven all his worst fears were justified, but that time had passed and the world had moved on, and indeed young Phil Bach had restored some sense of honour after the disgrace that had befallen the club. In its wake Lieutenant Colonel Gibson-Poole and Mister Walker had their own consciences to live with, and it was not Ossie Cochrane's place to pass comment. And it was probably true that his own sporting philosophy belonged to a different age. He looked around the ground from the high terraces in front of him to the main North Stand, with the distinctive curved roof, to the Holgate End and the twin-tiered South Stand.

'Of course we needed somewhere to play, though we never imagined anything so grand,' the old gentleman

The young Tom Bach. 'A genuine leviathan.'

There was an alternative or two for watching the game if you did not want to fork out for the 3d admission price. This was one way…

sighed. 'After our falling out with Mister Kemp, we realised we needed to find somewhere more permanent than a farmer's field. You see, we never dreamed anyone would want to come and watch! Yet by the end of the century that is what was happening. Thousands of them. And many of them quite common people…'

He smiled to himself. In the end it was because the so-called common people had taken such an enthusiastic interest in it that the game had outgrown its humble beginnings. Whether or not it was a good or a bad thing was for other people to judge. In either case, there was no turning the clock back. Ah, but if he could…

It had been fortunate that, as a player himself for the Tees Wanderers Rugby Club who used the ground, along with those other gentlemen such as Mister Hardisty, Mister Ewbank and so forth, who were members of the cricket club that adjoined it, they had known about the rugby field. And even more so that together they had some influence with the occupier. In the earliest days when the Archery Ground had served as their home they had of course considered the field on Linthorpe Road, but cost and circumstances had been against them. But by the early months of 1880 things had changed somewhat, and there were enough spectators prepared to pay their threepence to watch the game, to make renting a permanent home a more viable proposition.

…or you could climb one of the trees at the Plantation End for a good view of the action. Middlesbrough town is in the distance.

The Linthorpe Road Ground from the Plantation End, looking towards the Village.

Although a Mister John Marshall, who rented it from the Middlesbrough Estate, occupied the field, Ossie Cochrane knew that the Wanderers had an understanding with this gentleman to allow them to play their games on the site, and he had been certain that something similar could be organised on behalf of the football club. Certainly until such time as they could establish an official arrangement with the estate themselves. The way things were going in regard to the attendances for matches, the payment of a small fee to Mister Marshall, certainly less than Mister Kemp was demanding for his field, would no longer present any difficulty at all.

It was still a far cry from the sort of stadium he would come to marvel at all those years later, but Ossie Cochrane had been pleased enough at the time with the solution to the difficulties presented to them by Mister Kemp. If he could not exactly bring himself to shake the farmer's hand as he and his fellows dug up their goalposts once again and prepared to move on, he consoled himself with the knowledge that a lesser man would have thumbed his nose at him.

And so, the Linthorpe Road Ground had become their home – a proper sport-dedicated field in easy reach of the town and the outlying district. There was even a public house right across the road, the Swatters Carr Hotel, though the old cricket and sports field of that name was now a building site. The Cleveland Agricultural Society had held their last annual show there as recently as the previous summer, but those days were over. The Grand Opera House was being built.

The Swatters Carr Hotel became the club's temporary headquarters and was ideally placed for the players to get changed in before and after games until such time as a dressing room facility was provided behind the goal at the Linthorpe Road end of the ground.

Things got up and running on 28 February 1880. Tyne Club of Newcastle were old friends by now and were the first visitors to the Linthorpe Road Ground. The Boro recorded a handsome 4–1 victory, but what was especially rewarding was that they achieved it in front of a very decent gathering of spectators. If the attendances were already measured in the hundreds it would not be long before they increased to more than 1,000. Especially after, just a year later, the Cleveland Association was formed in the Swatters Carr Hotel, amid much celebration, and the Cleveland Cup competition was inaugurated, bringing with it the opportunity for a local tournament that would be a true test of proper competitive sportsmanship.

By the summer of 1882 Middlesbrough Football Club had made the Linthorpe Road Ground their own and had completed a formal agreement with the estate to rent the land. In 1884 there was great excitement at the building of a grandstand on the northern side of the ground to go with the dressing rooms, offices and stables that now occupied the north-eastern corner. Access to the ground was either along the footpath, which would later become Clifton Street, along the northern side of the ground, or by one of the turnstiles by the main entrance on Linthorpe Road itself.

By now some of the founder members of the playing staff were becoming a little long in the tooth. Fred Hardisty, for instance, was still hard at work but at an administrative level, a fervent adherent of amateurism. Charles Booth would continue as a player in the early 1880s, and the likes of Ossie Cochrane himself, even after assuming the role of chairman of the club, and Jackson Ewbank (despite a serious injury incurred on the cricket field) would continue right up until the late 1880s, only hanging up their boots for the last time as the prospect of football in the new Northern League presented itself. But there was a steady supply of up-and-coming youngsters ready to replace the old guard. Albert Borrie was already a goal-getting revelation, joining Jeremiah Dawkings and Billy Pickstock as one of the star attractions, along with even newer faces: Toby Wynn, Dave Mullen and 'a young leviathan' called Tom Bach, who would make his debut in October 1886 in a 1–0 FA Cup victory over Bishop Auckland. While Toby Wynn would take on the captaincy as the Northern League began, Tom Bach would inherit the role in due course and, along with his brother Phil, had a major role to play as events unfolded during the late 1890s. In different ways and for different reasons the club would owe much to both men.

The view you would have got looking over the fence from Linthorpe Road towards the Plantation End.

But before that there was another battle to be won, against opposition that emerged right on the doorstep of Middlesbrough Football Club in the hallowed environs of the Swatters Carr Hotel. Trouble had been brewing since Ossie Cochrane's deciding vote retained the amateur status of the club in 1886. Three years later the storm broke. And its name was Ironopolis.

Ironopolis

'You fellows should be paying me to do this!' said Alfred Mattison, speaking only half in jest.

He had just scored a decisive goal, adding to the two that Albert Borrie had scored as Boro won the Cleveland Cup for the second time, 3–2 against Redcar on 24 March 1883.

He played for Middlesbrough in their very first Cleveland Cup game, a 9–0 victory over Guisborough, in January 1882, and scored the winner in the Final of the same competition. If he only made a handful of appearances since then, they were notable and included scoring a hat-trick against Loftus in November

In 1888, the same year as the Football League began, Jack the Ripper was terrorising London, while a dagger of a different type was about to slice across the heart of the Boro.

of that year. His last appearance was the second Final against Redcar, and like Cochrane and Hardisty before him he became a director of the club, but unlike those stalwarts of the amateur game he adopted a rather different philosophy.

The way forward, as Alfred Mattison saw it, was in the competitiveness of a professional League financed with public support.

'Look,' he said. 'It's already happening in Lancashire and the Midlands!'

Even though professionalism had been legalised in July of 1885, it was not until 1888 that the Football League was established. And it is probably fair to say that we have Aston Villa Football Club to thank for it. Their first honour had been the Birmingham Challenge Cup in 1880 (at which time, their captain, a certain Mister George Ramsay, with possibly too much time on his hands used to make his own long-flannel pants to wear during games). Then, in 1887, having won the FA Cup, their director, William McGregor had the bright idea that a 'Football League' might be quite a lucrative venture. As he settled down on 2 March 1888 to contact at first just five clubs, he was effectively isolating the amateur football teams of the South in favour of the newly formed professionals in the North. Eventually, Accrington, Blackburn, Bolton, Burnley, Everton, Preston, Aston Villa, Derby County, Notts County, Stoke, West Bromwich and Wolverhampton were invited to form a professional League. As Oswald Henry Cochrane had already noted, in the North some quite common people were changing the face of the game forever.

The men behind the northern teams were industrialists, small businessmen, the working classes, and the split became inevitable. The southern gentlemen had played their part, but the game was evolving and in Middlesbrough the change was noted.

Mattison said: 'We have to acknowledge that this is the way the game is going. We don't want to be left behind.'

There were young men in the team who could not play forever, and not all of them had a public school education to fall back on. Why should they be criticised for wanting to be paid for the entertainment they were providing? They were seeing less-talented footballers making a living for themselves and their families and surely could not be blamed for wanting to do the same? In 1886, the matter had been addressed but, thanks to Mister Cochrane's casting vote in favour of amateurism, dismissed. It was not going to end there though, and it all came to a head in October 1889.

Middlesbrough Football Club were not enjoying the best of times as it was. Just as the Football League had got underway a year earlier, the Northern League had been inaugurated and the Boro were among the original members. An opening day victory, 3–2 over Elswick Rangers, had been downgraded to a draw after it was discovered that Boro had fielded an illegible player and, followed by defeats against Newcastle East End, Stockton and St Augustines, along with an FA Cup exit at South Bank, it meant that they were struggling as winter set in. There was unrest in the team, and it was contributing to poor performances. The events of 29 October did nothing to help when a meeting in the Temperance Hall in Middlesbrough passed a resolution to allow the formation of a new football club in the town. A professional football club.

Alfred Mattison had got his way and was quick to search out Middlesbrough players Billy Hopewell, Jack Taylor and Tom Cronshaw, whom he knew would be delighted with the news. He met up with them in the Swatters Carr Hotel and insisted they got wrapped up warm and come and join him in his pony and trap because there was something he wanted to show them. They rattled along, passing the Linthorpe Road Ground, all grey and gloomy under an overcast sky, not travelling far. Only half a mile or so. As they reached the main gates of Albert Park, Mattison turned the trap right and, after guiding it a short distance over the uneven ground of a farm track, brought it to a halt. Oldgate Farm was to their right, and ahead of them, over the low ground, was the Union Workhouse and the Methodist Chapel, the Paradise Mission. In-between, next to where they had stopped was an open field, much of it water-logged.

'There you are, lads,' said Alfred Mattison. 'That's your new home if you sign up with us. It'll need to be drained, of course, being such low-lying land, but everything is arranged.'

'It's going to happen then?' Hopewell could hardly believe it.

'Oh, yes, Bill. They're selling shares in the new company at one pound a time. We're fitting up the field there for matches. We'll have the stands up before Christmas!'

'And they're going to pay us to play football?'

'Better sign up while you still can, lads. They're advertising for players right now, and they'll get hundreds wanting to be a part of it! You'll be captain if you make your mind up quickly, Billy. I can't think of a better man to uphold the honour of the town.'

Hopewell, Taylor and Cronshaw were on board. They walked out on Middlesbrough Football Club in December and joined the new outfit that, on 18 November 1889, had been christened Middlesbrough Ironopolis Football Club. They took the name of their ground from the Mission that had previously rented it and it became the Paradise Ground. By December it was ready. The standing water had been drained and, though the ground still resembled more of a quagmire than a football field, it was ready for play. It had been fenced around and a path had been lain down to provide access for the thousands of spectators that the new club expected. They even got the two stands up in time.

The defection of their players was a blow that stirred the Boro. A draw at home to Darlington and a defeat, 4–2 against Birtley, with Tom Cronshaw scoring one on his final appearance before joining Ironopolis, were ample pieces of evidence that the Northern League was not going particularly well for them. But they were about to discover they still had some fire left.

On 7 December they hosted Sunderland at the Linthorpe Road Ground in a friendly fixture that might not otherwise have been noteworthy, not least because they lost again, 3–0, had it not been for one important feature. They had turned professional themselves. And had beaten Ironopolis to playing the first professional match in the town by seven days. It had been the only way to stop more players walking out on them and the disaster that would have followed. On 14 December, while Middlesbrough FC succumbed to a 7–0 humiliation away to Darlington (oh yes, it got worse before it got better), Ironopolis were enjoying a 1–1 draw in their first game at the Paradise Ground against Gainsborough Trinity. It was too far on in the season for them to achieve much in 1889–90, except arrange as many prestigious friendly games as they could, and they set their sites on the next campaign, in the Northern League.

For Middlesbrough FC, enough was enough.

Possibly because the factions no longer existed that had compromised team spirit, things improved on the pitch. And off it too. The Ironopolis players even deserted their old watering hole, the Swatters Carr Hotel, and shifted their allegiance to the County Hotel on Newport Road, while Boro won at last, beating Elswick Rangers 4–0 away from home with four new players making their debuts: Bill Barbour was the new goalkeeper and would go on to become club trainer, and joining him were Stevenson, Petrie and McGregor, who scored twice. Toby Wynn was still captain, and Tom Bach, the captain-in-waiting, rallied the troops to such an extent that they went on a winning run to turn the season round. There were rumours in the town that Tom was on his way to Ironopolis too, especially when an R. Bach was named as their trainer, giving rise to the speculation that family loyalty might override club loyalty. But Tom stayed with Boro and became captain in due course and had a hand in persuading his younger brother Phil to come on board too for the 1893–94 season. St Augustines won the Championship, but Middlesbrough steadily improved and only lost twice more, gaining some consolation by winning the Cleveland Cup.

The last sentiments should be expressed by Fred Hardisty: 'It's not possible to overestimate the damage that the split caused. At that point we were becoming a force in the game. We had played against the likes of Old Etonians, Blackburn Olympic, both FA Cup winners and suchlike, and on each occasion given as good as we got. If we had stayed together, who knows what we might have achieved. Nowadays people talk of Preston North End as the Invincibles, but I can't help thinking of what might have been.'

Boro captain Mister Toby Wynn shows off the kit that Boro favoured in the 1889–90 Northern League season. Odd that it never caught on!

Ironopolis v Middlesbrough
There can be only one.

Once you get into a fight there is no backing down, and the two Middlebrough teams duly locked horns and set about throwing some serious punches. The green-and-maroon halves of Ironopolis versus the white with blue-and-white polka dots of Middlesbrough.

If nothing else, it was exciting. The Northern League of 1890–91 went right down to the wire. Early in the campaign, on 1 November, the first League derby took place at the Linthorpe Road Ground in front of 12,000 spectators and ended in a 2–2 draw. Middlesbrough may have been feeling the effects of their record-breaking performance of a week or two earlier when they had seen off Scarborough 11–0 in the FA Cup (at Scarborough).

Honours even then with Ironopolis but the battle joined. They were still head-to-head as the season drew to a close, and the deciding game was between the two rivals on 28 March 1891 at the Paradise Field. Ironopolis won 1–0. A collective groan went through the ranks of the men from Linthorpe Road. They missed out on the League title by one point.

It was the same story next time round, Ironopolis champions and Middlesbrough runners-up. On Boxing Day 1891, Ironopolis beat Boro at the Paradise Field then completed the double a few days later, just after the New Year. They then underlined their superiority by winning the Cleveland Cup 4–0, vanquishing the Boro in a competition they had once dominated.

In the close season that followed, things went on behind the scenes because the directors of both clubs had their eyes on the Football League. Better opposition meant better crowds. Attendances had fallen, with only the derby games between Boro, Stockton and Ironopolis attracting local interest, and the only other decent attendances were for FA Cup ties against opposition from a higher level. The Invincibles of Preston North End, for example, had created a stir when they came to town in January 1892, having walloped Ironopolis in the first round 6–0, they faced a much sterner challenge against Middlesbrough, who only just went down 2–1 in front of nearly 10,000 spectators.

There remained an obvious problem of two Middlesbrough teams vying for election to the Football League when votes for applicants were not exactly easy to come by.

Fred Hardisty and Albert Borrie, as chairman and club secretary respectively (in one of Mister Hardisty's last acts in the position), could attest to the truth of this. They had applied on behalf of their club to join the Football League and received only one vote in support.

But then someone had a bright idea: 'What if the two teams merged?'

The meeting was arranged in the Odd Fellows Hall in May 1892, and it might have happened. In fact it very nearly did. Everything was agreed, in principle. A

The battle for survival.

disgruntled murmur or two here and there but nothing that could not be sorted out. Until they came to the thorny question of what to call the united club. Just think, if they'd thought of the simple name 'Middlesbrough United' we might have an even richer history, if such a thing is possible, than the one we now enjoy. Instead, one half wanted 'Middlesbrough Ironopolis Football Club Limited' and the other insisted on 'Middlesbrough and Ironopolis United Football and Athletic Club Limited.'

It was the end of negotiations and the two bodies went their separate ways into the night.

Mister Hardisty, on behalf of Middlesbrough FC, subsequently turned down a Football League invitation to join the new Football League Division Two on the grounds that the opposition, in his opinion, could not be deemed attractive enough. Before adding, as much to himself as anyone else, 'I'm really getting too old for all this'.

1892–93 was the worst season that anyone could remember for Middlesbrough Football Club. The crowds drifted away. Ironopolis dominated yet again, and Tom Bach growled into his beer, which at least he did not have to pay for (he had taken over ownership of the Masham Hotel, near the Railway Station [It's still there; I think it was a shoe shop last time I looked.]). He dashed off a note to be sent round to his brother Philip. Like Tom, he had relocated with the rest of the family, from Ludlow in Shropshire to Middlesbrough, as a child and had grown up to become a keen sportsman. The note read something like this:

'Half the players are drunk, even during games. Roberts was supposed to be our captain but was never sober and abused the directors, with some quite colourful descriptions. He then vomited in Mister Taylor's bowler hat, and that might have been the last straw. I believe Mister Borrie showed Roberts the door and we haven't seen him since. Fall the goalkeeper and Abrahams are no better, and I believe they'll be the next one's out. There are good lads here though and with the right influence might do very well. Once again, old fellow, I urge that you come along and at least see if you can get a game. I believe there is a real opportunity here for the right man.'

The only compensation, in a clutching-at-straws kind of way, was that the Boro beat Newcastle United twice, 4–0 in the Northern League and 3–2 in the FA Cup.

Meanwhile, on Merseyside.

Founded as St Domingo FC in 1878 so that Methodist Churchgoers could keep fit during cricket's winter break, the club was renamed Everton FC after the surrounding area so that non-parishioners could participate. They wore blue-and-white stripes, but, as new players arrived still wearing their previous club strips, there was a confusion of colours on the pitch during games. Middlesbrough had faced the same situation in their earliest days and, rather than suffer the expense of a whole new kit, Everton found the same solution as the Boro came up with and all the shirts were dyed black, to which was added a scarlet sash. Between 1878 and 1892 games were played at Anfield Road, on a

Ironopolis 1 Middlesbrough 0 on Boxing Day in the Northern League 1891–92, at the Paradise Field, against the backdrop of the Union Workhouse, close to where the Holgate End would one day stand.

'Honest' John McKenna.

field owned by a brewer, John Orrell. John Houlding, the leaseholder, purchased the ground from Orrell and increased the rent from £100 to £250 a year.

The Evertonians objected and moved out to build a new home, Goodison Park, leaving an empty ground, just three playing members and their new blue-and-white halved shirts behind. Houlding decided it was all worth hanging onto and formed his own club.

'Honest' John McKenna, a selfmade Irish business man and former rugby player (he would become the Football League's longest serving president from 1910–36) and friend of Houlding, was appointed manager and filled the team with Scots. Names like, McClean, McCartney, McBride, McVean, the McQueen brothers, McOwen, McQue, earned them the nickname: 'Team of the Macs.'

On 15 March 1892 there may or may not have been a conversation at the Football Association at 61 Chancery Lane, London, that went something like this:

FA: 'So, Mister Houlding, you're applying to join the Football League?'

John Houlding: 'Yes. That's the general idea. I've paid for stands and I've appointed a team manager, Mister John McKenna. He's away in Scotland right now, recruiting players.'

FA: 'Excellent. Just what we like to hear. And what do you propose your team's name should be?'

JH: 'Well, at the moment we're Everton Football Club and Athletic Grounds Limited.'

FA: 'Bit of a mouthful, don't you think?'

JH: 'We could shorten it…'

FA: 'Now you're talking.'

JH: '…to Everton Athletic.'

FA: 'Are you trying to be funny? We've already got an Everton FC. Founder members of the League from '88. They've just won the First Division title, in case you hadn't noticed.'

JH: 'OK. What about…Liverpool Football Club?'

FA: 'Welcome to the Football League, Mister Houlding.'

And what has all this to do with us? Well, it just so happens after Accrington pulled out at the last minute that Middlesbrough Ironopolis in July of 1893 had successfully applied to join the Football League and their first home game was against Liverpool.

As has been said before the story of one club is the story of every club. And there are other connections too.

Liverpool were all set for their Second Division debut. Their new signing, James Stott from Middlesbrough, must have suppressed a shudder when he saw who the opposition was going to be. Middlesbrough Ironopolis. In effect it was a brand new Ironopolis with only skipper Duncan McNair retained from their Northern League incarnation, wearing their new cherry red-striped shirts, but the Paradise Field was still a familiar battleground for James Stott.

He played his part and Liverpool won 2–0. Malcolm McVean and Joe McQue got the goals, and if James was not on the scoresheet he made up for it with a hat-trick in the return at Anfield in October when Liverpool won 6–0, and he went on to become the club's top scorer that season, a highlight in his brief Merseyside career.

The season ended with Liverpool unbeaten, promoted to Division One after a Test Match 2–0 victory over Newton Heath, who finished bottom of the higher division (sadly, those two teams still hate each other over 100 years later, even after Newton Heath changed their name to Manchester United). Whether James Stott ever had a sneaky look to see how his old club, Middlesbrough, were doing is not recorded. But he must have cared a little bit because he actually returned in September 1899 for one last appearance in his old white shirt.

As regards those colours that we now know and love the Merseysiders in, it was soon afterwards, in 1894, that Liverpool eventually threw away the faded blue-and-white strip, which must have been more than a little moth eaten by then, and changed to red.

Everton were still lacking their own distinctive look though, trying out salmon pink shirts with blue shorts, then ruby shirts with dark blue shorts, switching, with a sigh of relief, to their famous royal blue shirts for the 1901–02 season.

A Season of Destiny
(1893–94)

In that same 1893–94 season, Middlesbrough won the Northern League for the first time (at last!), which was quite an achievement because they had done so

September 1893.
Ironopolis at the
Paradise Ground face
Liverpool (in the blue-
and-white halves), in
the Football League.

badly the previous year. Added to which, the rivalry with Ironopolis had adversely affected both clubs, and attendances were split between the attractions of Football League games at the Paradise Field and the unpredictable form of Boro at the Linthorpe Road Ground.

In the end, it was Ironopolis who came off worse. And it was not all down to themselves. Their season in the Football League did not really go all that badly. But the simple truth was that they simply could not afford to carry on. The high rent of the Paradise Field was one thing, the wages of the players another, along with the costs of travelling, and then there had been the calamity that had befallen them in November 1893.

Ironopolis had been beaten 6–2 by Grimsby Town at the Paradise Field, blaming the low attendance on the Boro's 'unsportsmanlike' behaviour in arranging a game against Bishop Auckland at the Linthorpe Road Ground on the same day (Boro lost 3–1, so that, according to the Ironopolis directors, should teach 'em). Then in the midst of all the disgruntlement the weather turned on Middlesbrough Ironopolis.

The *Athletic News* of 20 November 1893 had a neat way of describing the events. Their correspondent waxed lyrical about 'the storm fiend' and showed the benefits of a classical education by going on to bemoan 'the raging combination between Rude Boreas and Jupiter Pluvius, which prevailed [apparently] throughout the whole of Friday night and all day on Saturday.' He even went on to bring the Moor of Venice into the equation, but that was pushing it a bit. The gist of it all was that the wind played havoc with the Paradise Field. Half of the stand on the northern side was found some distance away in an orchard, while the larger covered stand had blown away completely. Funds were already badly depleted and the last thing they needed was the expense of erecting new stands. It was just another blow on the way to extinction.

The last rites for Middlesbrough Ironopolis were performed in June 1894. Alf Mattison, however, was not finished yet, and five years later he returned as a director to Middlesbrough, still dedicated to his dream of a professional team playing in the Football League. Middlesbrough FC should have been in every bit as much difficulty as Ironopolis. But they had addressed their own problems slightly differently by reverting to amateurism. At least it meant they did not have to pay the players. Although they lost several professionals (among them, Jimmy Stott as we have just seen), their form improved. Tom Bach stayed loyal, and his younger brother Phil had accepted his brother's invitation to join the fight and was among the replacements ready to take on the best that the Northern League had to offer.

It was the best thing that the club could have done. Not only did they win the League and regain the Cleveland Senior Cup, their new status meant that there was glory of a different kind just around the corner.

James Stott joined Liverpool from Middlesbrough.

Liverpool goalscorers McVean and McQue.

So, where's the Cup?

At some unspecified time in the 1880s the cloisters of Oriel College, Oxford University, echo with the thunder of expensive shoe leather on concrete paving slabs. Shadows flit between the archways that border the path to the Halls of Residence, and the summer sun lights up the afternoon.

'Hey, Charles!' cries one of the fellows as they race by.

His attention has been caught by the dapper young man seated by the open window of his chambers on the second storey of the building. The young man puts down his book and looks fondly down at his friend.

'I say! You aren't going to spend all afternoon with your head stuck in a book are you?'

A couple of others have also paused breathlessly beneath the open window.

'Come on, Charles,' another pipes up. 'We're all off for a game of rugger! Always room for one more!'

Charles Wreford-Brown smiles, then stretches himself lazily.

'By 'rugger' I assume, you blighter, that you are referring to the Rugby rules form of the game of football?' he says.

'I should say so! Employing the diminutive, don't you know?'

'Indeed I do, young Meriweather and no reason why you shouldn't.' He pauses, dreamily closing his book. 'However, blight-on-the-species that thou art, you should know that I have come to favour the Association rules of the game.'

'Come again? Afraid I didn't quite catch that last bit!'

'Very well, Meriweather. If you would be so kind as to allow it and since you

have led the way, please allow me to employ the diminutive also, if it will enable you to more easily understand?'

Noses wrinkle and mouths gape, not entirely gormlessly – these are Oxford fellows after all.

'I prefer to play, 'asoccer,' says Wreford-Brown. 'Now get thee to a nunnery. Or the rugger field, if you prefer.'

'I say!' chorus the fellows. 'That ain't fair! We won't forget this, Wreford-Brown!'

'Nice to be remembered for something,' comes the reply as the window quietly closes.

Just a month after Ironopolis's first Football League game, on 7 October 1893, Phil Bach scored on his debut for Boro in the Northern League against Stockton as the club's fortunes started to rise.

A word or two, then, about Charles Wreford-Brown, the man who first came up with calling this most hallowed of sports, 'soccer.' He was an amateur sportsman to the very depths of his being, though it always helps when you do not need the money, and his privileged background ensured that such was the case. He adhered to the purity of the 'noble athletic spirit', a flame that burned brightest without the 'corrupting influence of money.' In later years, when professional players and amateurs played together for England, Wreford-Brown always rewarded a goalscorer, if he was from the professional ranks, with a gold coin. He was a man of unimpeachable honour, as Middlesbrough Football Club would one day discover. Most relevant of all, he sat on the Council of the Football Association from 1892 to 1937. He played football for Old Carthusians, an exclusive club for ex-Charterhouse boys, and also for Clifton Association and Corinthians. Oh, and he was captain of the England national team in 1894 and 1895, which was the year that Middlesbrough Football Club rose to glory. In the 1894–95 season, as well as retaining the Northern League title, after victories over Bishop Auckland, Darlington (it needed two replays), Old Brightonians and the Lancaster Regiment, they won the Final of the FA Amateur Cup. It was a new competition, just a year old, and the fine gleaming trophy was held by Old Carthusians.

Ex-Charterhouse boys did not give up their trophies easily, and it was no surprise, least of all to themselves, when they reached the Final again. Middlesbrough hardly seemed like they presented very much of a threat. It might even be regarded as a little bit impertinent if they turned up at all. Except…a lesson had been learned by the Teessiders.

It was all very well saying, as John 'Allgood' Goodall of Preston's Invincibles, said: 'There is no game which is more calculated to raise the evil passions than football. Therefore a great deal of restraint and self control are absolutely necessary. A player must not regard it as a personal insult if the ball is taken from him or if he is the victim of a charge which, if heavy, is nevertheless legal. One might just as well expect a batsman to cherish a bitter hatred for the fieldsman who has just caught him brilliantly.'

Twelve years earlier, when Middlesbrough first entered the FA Cup (Old Carthusians were holders of that too at the time), the mining town of Staveley from Derbyshire had been their opponents at the Linthorpe Road Ground when the Middlesbrough team still comprised footballers who were drawn from the middle classes and who might have looked down on the other team, just a little bit. Big mistake. It had been such a bruising encounter that several Boro players were hospitalised afterwards, and Staveley won the game 5–1. But the lesson learned was to respect the spirit of the underdog. 'Allgood' Goodall's words were just fine and dandy, but sometimes you had to roll up your sleeves and get stuck in.

In other words, a new breed of rougher, readier footballers had emerged to take on the old guard. Middlesbrough Football Club was ready for Old Carthusians.

Wreford-Brown himself was injured and could not play, but Old Carthusians (in addition to impeccable breeding) still had Smith and Stanbrough, both England internationals, while Middlesbrough were led by Tom Bach, now in his 10th season at the club, and 10 other good men.

Headingley, 27 April 1895.

It started predictably. Gilbert Smith put Old Carthusians ahead, and as polite applause rippled through the crowd and amid handshakes all round no one noticed Tom Bach gritting his teeth. Maybe he was thinking of his younger brother Phil, unable to make the Final because of a broken hip, or maybe he had heard the whisper going around that the Charterhouse Old Boys were so certain of victory that they had not even bothered to bring the Cup with them. Whatever the motivation, he rallied the troops, encouraged those that needed it, cajoled and bullied where he had to and urged the lads on. Perhaps he even said: 'The drinks are on me back at the Masham if we pull this one out of the fire!' It did the trick anyway. Dave Mullen equalised. If there was a brief stunned silence from the spectators, it was instantaneously submerged by a full-throated roar of delight from the travelling Teesside contingent.

Tackles flew in. There was no more polite chatter from the stands. All eyes were on the pitch, on the blue-and-red hoops wilting beneath a thunderous white shirted charge. Then Alf Nelmes got the winner for Middlesbrough and the cheers were deafening. It is said that Wreford-Brown, watching from the stands with a gleam in his eye, applauded as enthusiastically as anyone. Whatever he thought of their tackling, he had to respect the Middlesbrough spirit.

They had earned their first major trophy. Except there was one thing missing. The trophy itself. As Tom Bach questioned the assembled dignitaries, goalscorers Mullen and Nelmes looked on. It was true then. Old Carthusians had had so much disrespect for their opponents they had left the trophy at home. The Boro team were incensed, and you can hardly blame them, but there was nothing for it but to head home with a promise that the Cup would be delivered in due course.

There were crowds to greet them at the Railway Station and a marching band too, and the spring sunshine never was so sweet. Tom Bach was true to his word, and the festivities in the Masham Hotel went on well into the night. But there would be no victory parade without the trophy, that was one thing all the players were agreed on. And that was the way it was.

Charles Wreford-Brown was not a man who was easily shamed. His own blameless life rarely gave him cause for embarrassment, but the whole business left a nasty taste in his mouth. He had seen evidence out there on the muddy

Headingley, FA
Amateur Cup Final, 27
April 1895. So, where
is the Cup?

field of his own true Corinthian spirit, and it had not been from the Charterhouse Old Boys. How could he make good the slight that the Teessiders had been dealt? He made a mental note that, should the day ever dawn that Middlesbrough Football Club needed a favour that it was within his power to provide, he would not be found wanting.

Things change in football and heroes are always moving on. Phil Bach joined Reading in the Southern League before signing for Sunderland in 1897. He enjoyed his first season with them, making 20 appearances as they finished runners-up in the Football League. In 1899 he won an England cap in a 13–2 victory over Ireland. Among his teammates that day was the Old Carthusian, Gilbert Smith who scored four times. As he congratulated the goalscorer, Phil said that he would have liked to buy Mister Smith a drink to celebrate his feat but that he had forgotten to bring a cup with him.

Phil almost rejoined Boro in 1901, but the transfer fee of £75 was a bit steep for the Linthorpe Road club, and it never quite happened. At this time

Phil Bach was already starting, like so many before him, to apply his talents at the administrative level. He played subsequently for Bristol City and Cheltenham Town before the curtain came down on his playing career. But there was a sting in the tail, and he was destined to return to Teesside one day. Older brother Tom gave up the game. The old warhorse had done enough, and he turned out for the last time in the early part of the 1896–97 season. He stayed on at the Masham Hotel for a while, though, and stayed in contact with his brother Phil. It turned out to be a good job that he did. And, as always, there were new heroes waiting to take their places on the field. It is about time we checked up on one in particular.

Bob Wanless

The last time we saw Bob Wanless he had just emerged into the world at about the same time, give or take a month or two, as Fred Hardisty was taking his tram ride to join Frederick Thompson and the others in the gymnasium behind the Albert Park Hotel for the meeting that would, quite literally, get the ball rolling.

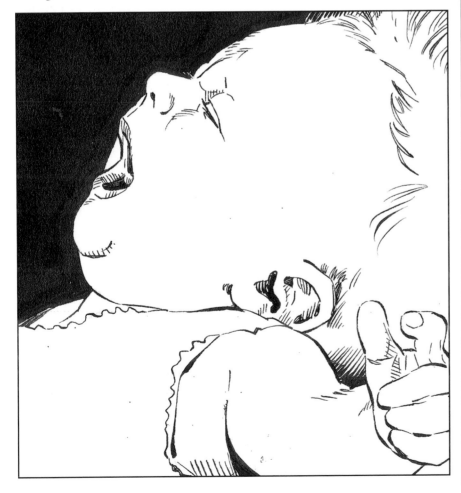

The last time we saw Bob Wanless he had just emerged, all pink and shiny into the world...

He had grown up a bit, just like the football club, by the time 1898 came around and was signed up by them to make his debut on the 26 March versus Leadgate Park. After a 2–1 victory he went on to have a decent enough career and was going to score one especially vital goal under rather odd circumstances. He would also appear in the team for Middlesbrough Football Club's very first Football League game, and that was not so far away any more. In fact it was just over a year away. He would be in and out of the team in that last season of his, but even afterwards he would still be seen faithfully following the club as a supporter. There will be another glimpse of him before we are done.

The Bach brothers had moved on. Who could possibly replace them? How about the Piercy brothers?

Frank Piercy

(1897–1904) 28 appearances.

Footballers who have turned out for both Boro and West Ham are few and far between, especially in those distant days of the early 1900s. But Frank Piercy was something of an exception. In 1897, 17-year-old Frank made his Boro debut in the Northern League, becoming more or less ever present in the 1898–99 season. He was the younger brother of team captain and fellow defender Henry Robert 'Bob' Piercy, who had been with the club since playing against Bishop Auckland on 15 September 1894 in the Northern League. Bob had been a loyal servant as a full-back, playing in that position through 1894–95, 1895–96, 1896–97, becoming captain in the 1897–98 season. He was a member of Tom Bach's legendary FA Amateur Cup-winning side of 1895 and was captain himself when Middlesbrough repeated the feat in 1898, as we are about to see. (And, typically Middlesbroughesque, it is not going to be straightforward.)

Frank Piercy's first game was as a centre-half on 4 September 1897, against Stockton in the Northern League, with Bob in the same team as captain. The younger brother played six games that season, though he missed out on an actual Amateur Cup Final appearance. In the 1898–99 season he played as a regular half-back or occasional full-back, missing only two games of that Final Northern League season.

When Boro joined Division Two in 1899, he made only two appearances (one in an FA Cup defeat to Jarrow) and then disappeared without trace along with his brother. As well as losing the captaincy, Bob played just eight times in the Football League, and it makes you wonder if lack of first-team games sent the brothers off in a bit of a huff.

Two years later, Frank resurfaced briefly, playing three games during 1902–03, Boro's last season at the Linthorpe Road Ground. He never made the move to Ayresome Park though, because in 1904 the great adventure was just beginning for the young blacksmith from Haverton Hill. He was on his way to another brand new

Opposite: Bob Wanless had grown up to be a footballer and rather a good one.

Frank Piercy in his West Ham colours and, years before, on his Boro debut against Stockton, 4 September 1897.

football arena as West Ham moved from the Memorial Ground in Plaistow to their new home in Green Street (Green Street House had once been the residence of Anne Boleyn, thus the surrounding area was more familiarly known as the Boleyn Ground). It must have seemed like crossing to the other side of the world when Frank set off to join them. He did not do badly either, playing 231 games for the Hammers, captaining the Southern League side and earning the nickname of 'the old warhorse.' After his retirement from playing in 1912, he became assistant trainer. By 1919, when he was not too busy in charge of the reserves, he also found time in his hectic schedule to play cricket and bowls for Essex and had a golf handicap of two. Not exactly Dick Whittington, but all the same…

This time, there had better be a Cup!

Now, about the rather odd circumstances that surrounded Bob Wanless's vital goal. It went something like this…

The dark days of the winter of 1898 were brightened up by Middlesbrough Football Club's inexorable progress through the early rounds of the FA Amateur Cup. It started on 29 January when Leadgate Park were sent packing 4–0, rubbing salt in the wounds of the same opposition that Boro had trounced 7–0 in the League just a week or two earlier.

February came and went, and if Northern League form suffered a bit, as in the 4–2 defeat to St Augustines, the Cup heroics stayed constant. After a 1–1 draw with Thornaby Utopians, the replay was won, 3–2. Robert Forrester was the chairman of the club, and he liked to take time in his busy life to stop by the Masham Hotel every once in a while and pass the time of day with his old friend Tom Bach, who had retired from playing earlier the previous season.

'We don't see you down at the ground very much these days, Tom,' said Forrester as he lit up his cigar.

The smoke curled through the hazy winter sunshine slanting through the nicotine stained windows.

'It's owing to the calls of my business, Mister Forrester,' replied Tom as he polished glasses behind the bar. 'I can't get away so often as I might like. I'm sure they're getting on just fine without me.'

In his shirt-sleeves he still looked every inch the strongman who had defied Northern League forward lines for the last decade or so.

'They're good enough, Tom,' Forrester took a sip of his drink. 'There's no denying it. I wouldn't put it past them to emulate your boys.'

'I wish them well, then. Just make sure there's a Cup for them to pick up this time.'

Someone coughed over in the far corner of the bar, and both men turned to see a man wafting the tobacco smoke away from himself.

'Sorry,' he spluttered. 'It's the smoke. That's all.'

Forrester nodded and turned back to his drink, exchanging a hard look with Tom Bach. The latter shrugged. There was nothing he could do about it if someone wanted to have a coughing fit. People were on edge, that was all. Ever since the first smallpox victim was diagnosed and the epidemic had taken a grip on the area, everyone was on their guard, watching for the first signs of any kind of illness.

'I never thanked you properly for the circus performance, Mister Forrester,' said Tom, changing the subject as quickly as he used to wrong foot opposing centre-forwards.

'What's that?' said Forrester. 'Oh, you mean Alvo's Circus. It was the least we could do. After all you did for the club. A benefit performance like that was our way of saying thank you.'

'Very much appreciated, I'm sure.'

'Do you miss it, Tom?' Forrester looked over his glass at his friend. 'When it's a fine day and you see the open field or hear the cheering crowd, don't you wish you still had your football boots?'

Tom Bach smiled grimly.

'I miss being young. Who doesn't? And the game is for the young, after all. Let them have it is what I say, and let them have as much fun with it as I did. I wouldn't wish things any different.'

And he winked at Robert Forrester and carried on cleaning glasses.

Boro beat the nomadic Casuals 1–0 on 26 February to reach the semi-final of the FA Amateur Cup. They were on the brink of glory yet again. And then fate stepped in to try and take it all away.

The other semi-finalists were Thornaby, with the game scheduled to be played in Darlington. The thing was that the smallpox epidemic was still rife on Teesside. It had not abated at all, and the last thing the population of Darlington wanted was for hordes of football supporters to carry the infection with them into County Durham. So they complained en masse to the Football Association, and the Football Association saw their point.

They immediately sent a telegram to Robert Forrester and the Board of Middlesbrough Football Club, which read as follows: 'Emergency Committee suggest that you scratch from the Cup semi-final in consequence of unfortunate epidemic. Matter considered serious. Trust in the best interest of the sport you will adopt this course.'

'They're telling us to pull out, Tom,' Forrester complained angrily to Tom Bach later that same day in the tap room of the Masham Hotel. 'And I've sent a telegram back saying we refuse to do so. But, if it comes to it, I don't see that we'll have any other choice. We can't play the game if the FA refuse to sanction it!'

'The FA, you say?' said Tom thoughtfully. 'Did you know that young Phil is a councillor now?'

'Your brother? Sorry, Tom, I wish Phillip well, of course I do. But it's not like he has any influence with the Association, is it? We need help today, not in a few years time. Where are you going now?'

Tom had come round from the bar and was struggling into his coat.

'Sorry, Mister Forrester,' he said as he opened the door to the grey, drizzling afternoon that was waiting outside. 'I just remembered something, or someone rather, who owes me a favour. I have to send a telegram of my own.'

Phil Bach had pursued his ambitions at the administrative level of the game. While still playing, he became one of the leading lights of the Association and served later not only as an FA Councillor but as president of the North-Eastern League, vice-president of the North Riding FA, had a seat on the International

Committee and the League Management Committee. In other words, he did alright for himself and made more than a few friends along the way. At the same time, there was someone else taking a keen interest in young Phillip's progress. A gentleman who had himself served as a councillor since 1892, who would go on to become chairman of the International Selection Committee and serve as vice-president of the Football Association itself. Someone who, like Phil Bach himself, had missed the 1895 FA Amateur Cup Final through injury. His name was Charles Wreford-Brown.

Brotton in Cleveland is a hill village where the Romans used to have a signal station. Pleasant enough in lots of ways and dearly cared about by its inhabitants, it nevertheless has a slightly unexpected claim to fame, as the events of 2 April 1898 would definitely indicate. It was just after lunchtime, and a sea fret hung over the narrow lanes of the little village, drifting over the rooftops and around the trees next to a gloomy field. In ones and twos men came out of the mist to gather uncertainly together, all with one thing in common. They were all carrying football boots. Which was a bit handy really, because sometime earlier someone had erected football posts in the field where they stood.

Slightly apart from the main group were two men, who had been there longer than the others, wrapped in their great coats and stamping their feet to keep out the cold.

'It's ridiculous, Tom!' Robert Forrester insisted, his breath clouding the air around him. 'You can't play a game in secret like this! We're all here out of respect for you. For everything you've done. Even the Thornaby lads. But it can't go on!'

Tom Bach appeared not to be listening. For the hundredth time he took out his fob watch and looked closely at the dial. The breath whistled between his clenched teeth. It was nearly 1 o'clock. Where were they? They should have been here half an hour ago.

Forrester was still agitated, not certain why he had obeyed Tom's summons to meet him out here in the wild hills of Cleveland. He was even more surprised to find that the Middlesbrough and Thornaby football teams had all received the same invitation and to a man, because of Tom Bach, had accepted it, one by one appearing in the designated area. But Tom's idea was ludicrous.

'What time did you get here?' Forrester hugged himself to keep warm. 'It must have been early. I presume it was you that put up the goalposts and marked out the pitch? I thought so. But it won't work, Tom! Playing the semi-final in secret might prevent the disease-riddled population from infecting another county, but the FA won't recognise the result, whatever happens! And why do you keep looking at your watch?'

'I'm waiting for someone,' Tom said quietly, straining his ears because he thought he had just heard a familiar sound.

'Who? Who else have you invited to this pantomime?'

'This'll be them now,' said Tom Bach.

He was certain of it. It had to be. Down the fog shrouded lane came the dull thud of horse hooves on the muddy track, the jingle of a harness and the creak of the coach behind. Its dark shape loomed up and came to a halt by the edge of the field as all heads turned to look. The carriage door opened and a man stepped down, looking back at the expectant faces, taking them in one by one before his eyes settled on Tom.

'Mister Bach?' he enquired and tipped his hat politely.

'That'll be me,' answered Tom and extended a handshake to the newcomer.

'I have a note here for you, sir,' said the stranger.

He reached inside his coat and handed Tom a small folded piece of paper. Tom glanced briefly at it, and a tight smile passed over his craggy face. Turning to the others, he said:

'I think you should be getting the game started, lads. Otherwise it'll be dark before you finish!'

'Tom!' Forrester's eyes were bulging. 'I've told you! They can't play the game. It would be pointless. The FA won't recognise it!'

'I'm sorry, sir,' the man from the coach interrupted. 'It's Mister Forrester, isn't it? Very pleased to make your acquaintance, sir. I must inform you that you are not correct though, if I may, and meaning no offence. The game is sanctioned, sir.'

'What? And who the devil are you?'

Even as Forrester was speaking, more men were emerging from the coach.

'We are the match officials, Mister Forrester,' said the man. 'If it pleases you, sir. You can hardly have a Cup semi-final without the appropriate authorities present. Mister Wreford-Brown's compliments to you, sir.'

Even Tom Bach laughed at the look that came over Robert Forrester's face. From bafflement, through incredulity, to joy. Still smiling, he handed the note to his friend and watched him while he read it. It said simply:

'Charles Wreford-Brown is in agreement that the game may go ahead with full Football Association support. His compliments to Mister Thomas Bach, and he trusts that his debt to that gentleman and his club is, at least, in some small measure repaid. Sorry I can't be there, Tom but am with you in spirit at least. Come on Middlesbrough! Come on Boro!'

'It's from your brother,' sighed Forrester. 'From Phillip.'

'So I gathered,' replied Tom. 'Come along now, Mister Forrester. We don't want to miss the kick-off.'

And there, as he links arms with Robert Forrester and disappears into the mist, is the last we shall see of Tom Bach, the leviathan of Middlesbrough,

and if it did not really happen exactly like that, well, it could have done and is true enough to the character of those involved to remain a worthy end to their story.

The game itself? Yet another thriller, if only witnessed by a couple of disinterested sheep and a passing tinker. Thornaby took the lead, which they held until half-time, but Middlesbrough had thawed out by the second half and came back at them. Bishop levelled and then, even as the lights were coming on in the houses of Brotton in Cleveland and darkness was descending on that quiet place, Bob Wanless, the man who was the same age as the club itself, grabbed the winner for the Boro.

The Final itself was held at the Crystal Palace in London on 23 April 1898, and Middlesbrough beat Uxbridge quite comfortably to win 2–0 in front of

Uxbridge 'keeper Gumbrell tries to throw the ball upfield, but it rebounds off Jim Kemplay into the goal.

Eddie Pugh is on the left, while Andy Ramsay is beaten to a header by the Bolton forward, and Boro goalkeeper Martin Hughes is scrambling for the ball.

2,000 spectators. Bishop scored one, and the other was credited to Jim Kemplay after the Uxbridge goalkeeper, Gumbrell, in trying to throw the ball upfield only hit the Boro forward in the face and it rebounded into the net.

As captain Bob Piercy looked anxiously around at full-time, he suddenly saw it. There it was waiting for him to collect. It was actually there this time. Even as he and his teammates approached, a shaft of sunlight broke through the clouds overhead and reflected gleaming on the carved surface of the FA Amateur Cup.

This is really where the curtain comes down on the days of amateurism. The club had learned the lessons of their previous attempt to turn professional and the town was more than ready to give its support. Impelled by the fact that their recent successes had seen players such as Kemplay, Moore, Jackson and Nelmes move on to pursue their careers elsewhere, it was clear that a professional outfit was better placed to hang onto good footballers, to attract better ones and to pay them a penny or two for their trouble as well. There would be just one more season in the Northern League before that adventure was over.

There were three vacancies in the Football League Division Two and, on 19 May 1899, at the Old Boars Head Hotel in Manchester, Middlesbrough were elected to one of them. On 2 September 1899 they made their Football League debut and, although they lost 3–0 away to Lincoln, for such as Bob Wanless who played that day it was a whole new beginning. For the chairman of the club it was especially gratifying. Robert Forrester had stepped down and been replaced by Alfred Mattison, whose dream had been lived all too briefly in the guise of Ironopolis before being realised five years later with Middlesbrough Football Club.

Blood Red

2 December 1899.

In 1874 a football club was formed in Bolton. Their headquarters, under the ministrations of the club president, the local vicar, was in Christ Church School. But, whenever that good man's back was turned, the players would 'wander' over to the nearby Gladstone Hotel, which gave the team its name, Bolton Wanderers, and also provided somewhat stronger liquid refreshment than the vicar possibly approved of.

In 1883 another early instance of football hooliganism afflicted their old ground at Pikers Lane when the referee, Sam Ormerod, was not only booed off the field but also pursued with hostile intent all the way to the railway station. Five years later, Bolton Wanderers were one of the founding members of the Football League but, in 1899, had suffered the ignominy of relegation to Division Two. This was just in time to come up against Middlesbrough Football Club as they enjoyed their first Football League season.

Middlesbrough had just thrashed Burton Swifts 8–1 and gained a hard-fought goalless draw against Gainsborough Trinity, so expectations were high as they travelled to Burnden Park on 2 December 1899.

'You're not going to wear those white shirts, are you?' someone asked the Middlesbrough players as they prepared for battle.

'That was the general idea,' Boro captain, McCracken, who had taken over the captaincy from Piercy, replied. 'Why? Is there a problem?'

The other man nodded towards the Bolton changing room where the home team were just emerging, ready to take to the pitch, resplendent in their own white shirts.

The goal came in the 88th minute, Alex 'Sandy' Robertson thumping the ball home in front of the Plantation End.

'I've got some red dye I could let you have the use of,' the man suggested, before adding 'for a very reasonable price.'

'Red?' spluttered Gettins, who had been with the club since 1893 and, though he did not play much any more, still liked to show his face every so often. 'We traditionally wear white shirts. Except for those couple of years we wore blue, obviously. But we can't wear bloody red!'

'Hold on,' said McCracken. 'Blood red. I quite like the sound of that.'

A crowd of just over 3,000 witnessed the historic occasion.

It was a bit like men against boys. Wanderers, on their way back to the First Division, had a greater experience that dominated the Middlesbrough side, eventually winning 3–0. But at least nobody could see you bleed. And Middlesbrough FC had found their true colours.

In only their third League campaign Middlesbrough won promotion to the First Division as runners-up to West Bromwich Albion. For their first home game at that level, on 6 September 1902, 20,000 people packed the Linthorpe Road Ground to see a 1–0 victory over none other than Everton FC. Boro had adopted the blood-red shirt now, and how it suited them as they took on the giants of the English game.

Chapter Seven

No Place Like Home: Ayresome Park

Middlesbrough v Sunderland

12 September 1903.

The Linthorpe Road Ground had been home for over 20 years. Even as the town expanded and grew around it, the old ground had continued to serve the club. But its days were numbered. The Middlesbrough Estate had already whittled away at the area available to the football club when they gave up part of it to the Reverend Selwood Godwin for the building of a church in 1898. Crowds were increasing. As many as 15,000 had been known to turn up just to watch pre-season practice games, and in the First Division as many as 20,000 might be expected to turn up. In 1900 the estate came up with a solution that they hoped would suit everybody. They had a plot of land adjoining the workhouse, in the Ayresome area, that they would lease to the club for an initial annual rent of £50. Yes, it would need to be drained as it was prone to flooding, being quite a low-lying area as Middlesbrough Ironopolis had once discovered, but in every other way it would appear to be an ideal situation for a brand new modern football stadium. But by the time of that inaugural season in Division One of the Football League, the new stadium had not been ready, and the club had to plead with the estate to hold onto the Linthorpe Road Ground for one more season.

'And here's £60 for the Reverend Godwin to stick into church funds if that helps at all…'

It did the trick, but just for one year more. The new ground had to be ready for the next season.

There were people in the crowd who remembered the fledgling club at the Archery Ground in Albert Park and Breckon Hill Road, even one or two who had played there. They took the name of the place from the ward where it was situated and called it Ayresome Park. It was built partly over the site of the Paradise Ground, home of the gone but not forgotten Middlesbrough Ironopolis. The 'Hollowed-out route' had been drained to create a playing area, and Archibald Leitch, the Glasgow engineer and football architect, had been commissioned to design the main grandstand, just as he would do for Arsenal, Manchester United, Chelsea, Everton, Liverpool, Tottenham and Aston Villa among many others, creating the look of Victorian Age stadiums that would survive well into the late 1980s. Tons of soil had been dumped to form the banks of terraces on three sides. Leitch himself had planned for these to be open areas, but the directors of the football club were determined to have at least one more covered area to complete the look of a modern stadium. It might have been a bit ramshackle, but it had served the club well, and the old North Stand from Linthorpe Road was dismantled piece by piece and brought by horse-drawn wagons to be re-erected as the official South Stand, the 'Little Stand,' at Ayresome. Just so long as the cameras were pointed at his own far more impressive new stand on the south side, Archibald Leitch let them get on with it.

Joe Cassidy scores the first League goal at Ayresome Park.

Labourers worked hard through the night right up to kick-off time so that those spectators who, having spent sixpence to get into the enclosure, then thought that it was a good idea to spend an extra ninepence to get into one of the stands, would have something to sit on. The sky was overcast, threatening rain. In those days, long before the boys end, Oldgate Farm stood at the north-eastern corner of the ground, and it might well have been the case that the Oldgate End faced the Holgate End, which might have been a bit confusing. As it was, they called them the Workhouse End and the Linthorpe Road End.

A pre-season friendly had seen the ground used for the first time as Boro beat Glasgow Celtic 1–0. That was on 1 September 1903, but the grandstand itself still had not been complete and was not open to the public. By 12 September workmen were still hammering away to get everything as near to being finished as they possibly could for the first home game of the 1903–04 season. In fact, they did not quite manage it, and part of the main stand was still under construction when the game kicked-off. The opposition was Sunderland, the Team of All the Talents. The smell of fresh paint and new timber was everywhere, except possibly in the rickety South Stand, which was by then in place and, like its illustrious neighbour, open for business, and everywhere was filled to capacity with 30,000 spectators cheering the teams on.

It seems appropriate that the first-ever League goal on the ground was scored by Boro captain Joe Cassidy at the Workhouse End. Countless more legendary goals would ripple the net at that part of the stadium later to be known as the Holgate. True, Gemmell equalised for Sunderland after the break, which the players had spent relaxing in the brand-new changing rooms that even had baths installed for their use, before Sandy Brown scored again for Middlesbrough. Unfortunately, things rather went downhill from there as Hogg and Robinson scored for the Wearsiders, who held on for a 3–2 victory. Still, the opening of the stadium was celebrated with a party that lasted well into the night. After all, it was the Edwardian Age where unbridled optimism was the rule of the day, and there was still a good 60 years or so to wait before *Match of the Day* came on. And at least the rain held off.

In the end it was not such a long wait for the first League victory at Ayresome Park. It was duly delivered on 26 September 1903 when Small Heath fell victim to a 3–1 mauling, courtesy of goals from Alex Brown and two more from Joe Cassidy.

A couple of years later...

On a bright winter morning in February 1905, the editor of the *Athletic News* periodical was spluttering into his bacon and eggs, barely able to articulate his outrage.

'What on earth is the matter, dear?' enquired his concerned lady wife, looking up from the pile of correspondence she was working her way through. 'I must say, you've gone a very funny colour!'

The gentleman composed himself with some difficulty and mopped his fevered brow.

'Haven't you heard the latest news?' he stared incredulous at his beloved, who was forced to admit that she had not.

'It's Middlesbrough Football Club! I can barely credit that what they've done is true! As you know, my dear, they are a club in some danger of relegation from the First Division to the Second. And what do you think they've gone and done about it?'

'I really couldn't possibly guess, darling.'

'Let me tell you then. They've only gone and spent...wait for it...and have the smelling salts handy... £1000, yes, you heard me right, £1000 on a player who they believe will score the goals that will get them out of trouble. It beggars

'...wait for it...and have the smelling salts ready...'

belief. I swear it does. I don't know what the world's coming to!'

'Oh, you mean that Alf Common person? Yes, they've acquired his services from Sunderland Football Club, I believe.'

'It's an outrage. Fancy spending all that money on a footballer just because he's better than the ones you've already got. Why, it's tantamount to cheating! Whatever you do, my dear, don't mention it when you correspond with your foreign friends, they'd think we've all gone mad!'

'Oh, don't worry, darling. I'm sure it's not the sort of thing that Mrs Abramovich would be interested in...'

Middlesbrough v Chelsea
1 January 1908.

On Boxing Day, 1907, Chelsea Football Club had beaten Middlesbrough Football Club 1–0. The game was played at Stamford Bridge, the old home of London Athletic Club since 1877 and which, in its first 28 years of existence, had

Sammy Cail puts Boro ahead against Woolwich Arsenal, 3 October 1908. Final score 1–1.

never witnessed so much as a single football game. That all changed when the brothers Augustus and Joseph Mears acquired the site and trusted Frederick Parker, a director of the London Athletic Club, when he put forward the notion that the place might very well be redesigned as a football ground. 'Think about it,' he said, 'if this was a properly designated football ground, then Fulham Football Club, who are renting the Craven Cottage site over there, might well be interested in something that was a bit more up to date. Fee to be negotiated, obviously.'

In addition it was not a bad idea to suppose that a ground capable of hosting a Cup Final, to say nothing of international games, was strategically located and especially built for the purpose, might be a quite sound proposition. With this in mind, they approached an architect whose work they admired. Archibald Leitch.

'Have you seen the North Stand that he designed for Middlesbrough?' asked Gus.

'A work of art,' agreed Joe.

(They had been on the point of pulling out of the project when Fulham turned down their offer to become tenants, but when Augustus's dog bit Frederick Parker's leg and the unfortunate gentleman took it so well, hardly wincing as the fangs sank in, they decided to trust his judgement after all. Chelsea Football Club, as a consequence, are probably the only team to owe their existence to a bad tempered Scottish terrier.)

The architect and Glasgow Rangers Supporter, Archibald Leitch, already had a reputation. He was the mastermind behind Ibrox in Scotland, a work of his in progress since 1899, and despite the tragedy at that ground when terracing collapsed, killing 25 people, had resurrected his own subsequently flawed

Alf Common heads the ball over the Chelsea 'keeper for Tommy Dixon to slide in and score.

Steve Bloomer was signed from Derby in April 1906.

Alf Common in action.

reputation with a commitment to solving the problems that had caused the disaster. At Sheffield United and Middlesbrough, which he delivered complete to his contractors for just over £11,000, the Mears brothers had observed his efforts and his grandstand design and innovative terracing that was a consequence of his determination that the tragedy of Ibrox should never be repeated. He was the man for them and, specifically, for Stamford Bridge.

With everything in place for their future success, the Mears brothers adopted the name of their newly founded club and its blue racing colours from Lord Chelsea.

On New Year's Day, 1908 approximately 30,000 people wrapped up warm and, shrugging off the winter chill, made their way to the Archibald Leitch-designed Ayresome Park to witness the debut appearance of the upstarts who, in their own very first top-flight season, had beaten the Boro on Boxing Day. After all, Middlesbrough Football Club had, by this time, been a First Division side since 1902 and in the Football League since 1899, and that defeat still rankled. But it turned out alright in the end.

Middlesbrough won 3–1 and, in the picture (on page 77), Alf Common (yes, he did eventually come good and score the goals that got Boro out of trouble) has just beaten the Chelsea goalkeeper to head the ball over for Tommy Dixon

to slide in and score one of his two goals, while Steve Bloomer (signed a year after Common and who had also contributed to the revival), scorer of Boro's other goal, looks on.

In the background, if you were in the Union Workhouse and made your way to one of the windows on the east-facing side, you could enjoy a free view of the game in much the same way as used to be provided by climbing one of the trees at the Plantation End of the old Linthorpe Road Ground.

The Return of Phil Bach

The editor of the *Athletic News* had expressed his previous outrage against Middlesbrough in print, and it had drawn attention to the club. In fact, Alex Mackie, the Sunderland boss who sold Alf Common to Middlesbrough, had soon followed the player to Ayresome Park and taken over as Boro manager. Which was a little bit of an odd coincidence. The Football Association warned that such high payments for players would be regarded as very poor form, so watch out, but despite this Middlesbrough, just a year after the Common outrage, were at it again. The £750 they spent on Steve Bloomer was hefty enough, even if it was not quite in the Alf Common league, and caused more than a suspicious glance or two being directed at the club. 'Where's the money coming from?' the people at the FA wanted to know. 'I thought they'd just announced a record loss of over £1000 for the 1905–06 season. Take my word for it, there's an element of dodginess about the whole thing.'

Of course, Ayresome Park attracted good crowds, which meant a nice pay day for visiting teams, but surely, the other First Division clubs wouldn't be swayed by that or be persuaded that, such being the case, they wouldn't want to see the club relegated and in order to prevent the aforementioned, a small loan might help them out. No need to mention it to the FA. But the FA had beady eyes and investigated. In May 1906 they announced that there was a whole catalogue of malpractices evident in what purported to be Middlesbrough's financial records. The club was fined £50 and warned that there was going to be a very close eye kept on them in future.

'I resign!' said Alex Mackie.

'Very good of you,' replied the FA. 'But we're suspending you anyway.'

Now, the incumbent chairman of Middlesbrough at that time was Lieutenant-Colonel Gibson-Poole, who was so fond of the club that he took personal charge of the weekly takings, and he consoled himself with the thought that at least the players they bought had done the trick and kept the club in the First Division.

The 1906–07 season had Andy Aitken in charge of team affairs as player-manager, and with 'Tiny' Tim Williamson in inspired goalkeeping form it was a rather more comfortable period. While the team continued to improve, there were still financial losses to be dealt with, although Lieutenant-Colonel Gibson-

As the *Titanic* sped to its doom...

Poole assured everyone that every penny was accounted for, and he should know because he took them home with him every night. Aitken was not happy about it at all, and by February 1909 had had enough. It is perhaps best not to speculate upon whether Gibson-Poole had tried to involve him in the same shenanigans he certainly inflicted on Andy Walker, his successor, and Aitken had refused to play ball.

John Gunter filled in for the departed manager, even though it was not his area of expertise, being a director of the club and more at home working with the steel industry, but he would do the best job that he could. He held the reins until 1910 when Andy Walker took over. By this time Lieutenant-Colonel Gibson-Poole had proudly ascended to the mayorship of the borough and, as he watched the team start the 1910–11 season so well that by December they were serious contenders for the Championship, he must have thought the world was smiling on him. This makes it all the more baffling that he did what he did, especially given the already dubious reputation the club had earned just a few years previously.

Lieutenant-Colonel Gibson-Poole, thinking how well the robes of elected office suited him, wanted more than anything else to be elected a Conservative Member of Parliament, and how could the town not vote for such a man who had delivered to them a football club that was on a winning run, whose players were out and about campaigning on his behalf? Let the Liberals do better than that if they could! There was a game coming up against Sunderland, and what a perfect opportunity it represented to put himself in an unassailable position. But, it was probably best to make certain – to be sure that nothing could possibly go wrong.

With that in mind, along with Andy Walker (whom he got to do his dirty work), he offered the Sunderland players a bribe to…well, to not quite give their all in the upcoming encounter. Unfortunately for the Lieutenant-Colonel and Mister Walker, Charles Thomson, the Sunderland captain, not only turned down the £10 he was offered, but he also reported the matter to his own board. They, in turn, went straight to the FA, who had just about had enough of the financial mismanagement, illegal payments to players (cooking the books was the least of it) and now attempts at bribery of Middlesbrough Football Club. It certainly cast a doubt or two regarding the good run the team had enjoyed since the start of the season, and even more so when, once the cat was out of the bag, form slumped dramatically and they finished in 16th place in the table (though they still beat Sunderland 1–0 in the game that started all the trouble). Lieutenant-Colonel Gibson-Poole and Andy Walker were hauled over the coals in no uncertain manner. Guilty as charged with no recommendation for clemency.

Middlesbrough Football Club was warned that any further misdeed would result in expulsion from the League, and as for the two guilty men, with capital punishment unfortunately not being an option (and too good for 'em, in lots of people's opinion), they would have to settle for being banned for life from the game, with the commission in particular condemning the way that Gibson-Poole had dominated the club. It had not been the best week of his life certainly, especially when the votes were counted and the Liberals won the Election rather emphatically.

…and sank into the icy waters it must have cheered the passengers enormously to know that Middlesbrough Football Club had regained its honour.

As the disgraced pair collected their belongings and trudged their separate ways homewards, a familiar figure was making his way in the opposite direction towards Ayresome Park. Newly elected to the board of directors and determined to restore some of the good name the club had once enjoyed, Phil Bach had returned to Middlesbrough. He had finished his playing career at Cheltenham Town and become a successful hotel proprietor and had recently purchased the Empire Hotel on Linthorpe Road, which is what they were calling the Swatters Carr Hotel in the early 1900s. He might have looked across the road and seen the terrace of shops between Princes Road and Gresham Road and fondly remembered the old football ground that had stood there, but just as likely he would have been determined to revive the fortunes of the club he remembered in its latest incarnation that had fallen so far into notoriety. And that is just what he did.

Phil was elected to chairman in 1911, a position that he held until 1925 and then regained in 1931 until 1933. The early days were possibly the most rewarding of all. He oversaw new terracing that was laid down in front of the North Stand and appointed Tom McIntosh as manager. As the Transporter Bridge was erected over the Tees in 1911, and in 1912 the *Titanic* sank into the icy waters south of the Grand Banks of Newfoundland, Middlesbrough Football Club steadily improved and finished as high as third position in the 1913–14 season.

The next season was not so good, but 12th place was not a disaster and hope was high that progress would continue. Then World War One broke out and everyone's dreams were put on hold.

George Washington Elliott

(1909–25) 365 appearances.

George Washington Elliott was in his first season as a Middlesbrough centre-forward when he scored the winner against Aston Villa on 28 March 1910, in a 3–2 victory at Ayresome Park. He is pictured in action battering the Villa defence against the East End of the ground. It was his second goal of the 213 that he would eventually score. He still holds the club record for most goals in a single game, 11 in a 14–1 win over Houghton Rovers for the reserve team. Before his retirement in 1925 he had bridged the generations of great players, from Steve Bloomer and Alf Common to the time when a young George Camsell was getting ready for the fray.

The goal against Aston Villa was especially praiseworthy. They won the Championship that season, reaffirming their place at the forefront of a game they had dominated in the late 1880s. From being runners-up in 1888, they were champions in 1894, 1895, 1896, 1897 (when they won the double), 1899 and 1900.

George Elliott went through a few striking partners during his time. Sammy Cail was one until he was transferred to Stalybridge Celtic in 1913, at which point a young man from Sunderland was starting to catch the eye. Enter Walter Tinsley.

Opposite: George Elliott takes on the Aston Villa defence on 28 March 1910.

Walter Tinsley slots home the penalty. He would be gassed in the trenches of World War One, but he recovered sufficiently to star for Nottingham Forest and Reading.

Walter Tinsley

(1913–21) 89 appearances.

A cold, wet Ayresome Park, 13 February 1915. Boro, 4–1 up at half-time, are hanging onto a 6–5 lead after a Spurs fight back. John Eadon, the Tottenham goalkeeper making one of only five appearances for the club, is wishing he had stayed at home as he faces a late Boro penalty. If Walter Tinsley feels any nerves at all he does not show it, and he slots the kick home to secure the points.

'One-a-week' Tinsley, nicknamed after his regular scoring habit, was a success with four clubs, yet is now a forgotten man. He signed for Boro from Sunderland in December 1913 and bagged 19 goals in 23 games as Boro finished third in Division One, and would score 49 altogether in 89 appearances. But, as he took that penalty against Spurs, the shadow of the Great War was already upon him.

Tinsley was Boro's top scorer in 1914–15 with 26 goals, but not until 1919, after hostilities ceased, would he get another chance. And by then everything had changed. In fact, he only scored four more over two seasons. The war took its toll. He had been gassed in the trenches, and there were teammates, including Andy Jackson, captain of the team that beat Spurs, who never returned home. So it is not surprising if some of the fire went out of him. Whereas George Elliott resumed normal goalscoring service immediately after the hostilities ceased, 'One-a-week' Tinsley was no longer the same player. He lost his regular place in the team and in 1921 moved to Nottingham Forest. Oddly, there is a blurry picture of him in a Forest line up at a Victory Shield match in 1918, two years before his official transfer from Boro.

Then, in 1925, he turned up in Division Three South with Reading. He was part of Championship-winning sides for all the clubs he played for, except one. Guess who? The nearest he came with Boro was that 1913–14 season. But who knows what might have been. Then again, a lot of people in the aftermath of World War One were saying 'if only…'

George Camsell

(1925–39) 453 appearances.

A young heathen called George Camsell, along with some equally ungodly miners of Framwellgate Moor, Co. Durham, was once caught by the local vicar playing football on a Sunday. The appalled cleric hauled the youngster from the pitch and demanded to know what he meant by it and what his poor father would say if he knew. George replied that he could ask him himself if he liked, because that was the old chap over there, playing in goal. Which just goes to show it is something in the blood, and that inherited skill was serving George well by the time that the 1926–27 season came around.

Having made his Boro debut the previous season, his career was really taking off by the time December came around. As the team set off to play away at Manchester City, he had already scored 26 times, including three hat-tricks, taking the Second Division by storm.

George Camsell.

Middlesbrough were leaders of Division Two, heading for promotion, and City were one of the challengers. George notched all five goals as Boro won 5–3 at Maine Road on Christmas Day, and a crowd of over 44,000 jam-packed themselves into Ayresome for the return fixture just two days later. A handful of police kept some kind of order as the barriers gave way, with hundreds thronging the touchline. It was a better view, however, if you clambered out of the crush up the groaning timbers to the top of the south stand.

It was called the 'little' stand and had stood on the south side of Ayresome Park since 1903. Hardly an imposing edifice opposite the Archibald Leitch designed main stand, the old Linthorpe Road stand had withstood gales and tempests. In fact, in roughly the same location, Middlesbrough Ironopolis Football Club lost both its stands to the weather in the winter of 1893, so, ramshackle though it might have been by 1926, the 'little' stand had served the Boro well; though it was creaking a bit on 28 December when Manchester City came to town.

The Little Stand creaked beneath the weight of spectators while the use of a ladder to get you to the roof would cost you a penny.

George Camsell on the left, scoring one of his trademark tap-ins.

The *Gazette* of the day speculated that access was at the back, where supporters were climbing the boards then being hoisted to the tiled roof by those already up there who hung down scarves and raincoats to help them. Personally, I would not bet against the likelihood that some entrepreneurial resident of Clive Road was renting out his ladder at a penny a go. My grandparents lived on Tavistock Street just around the corner, and I like to imagine them earning themselves an extra shilling or two that way.

It all ended happily, with Camsell scoring twice in a 2–1 victory, then being chaired off the pitch by the triumphant hordes. It is highly likely that the apoplectic priest from Framwellgate Moor was not among them. Indeed, he would probably have long since given up on young George, but he might have paled just a little if he had seen the date for that Maine Road fixture: it was Christmas Day, 1926. As if playing football on a Sunday was not bad enough! The 'little' stand survived the experience too and would remain until 1936 when it eventually succumbed to its own antiquity.

In 1926–27, George Camsell scored 59 of Middlesbrough's 122 goals as they became champions of Division Two. Peter McWilliam had taken over as manager in the latter part of the promotion campaign but was unable to work any magic the following season as the team was immediately relegated. (Camsell himself contributing a measly 37 goals!) And to make matters worse, ex-Boro target Dixie Dean's record of 60 goals from 39 League games in 1927–28 for Everton beat Camsell's achievement of just the previous year. Had Middlesbrough forked out the £2,000 that Dean's previous club Tranmere were asking for him back in 1924, it might have been a different story.

Promoted again, as champions, in 1928–29, Boro then established themselves in the top division. The picture (on page 87) shows a scene from the game at Highbury on 16 November 1929. This was a time when Arsenal and Chelsea were the only teams to wear shirt numbers (they became compulsory in 1939). Arsenal's distinctive white sleeves made their appearance in the 1930s as the team started to do rather well for itself.

George Camsell is on the left in the white shirt, scoring one of his trademark tap-ins as Boro beat the Gunners 2–1 (the other goal was scored by Ernie Muttit on his debut). Billy Pease is the Boro player in the background, while the Arsenal player on the right is David Jack, the first man to score in a Wembley Cup Final, who had been bought from Bolton to replace Charlie Buchan the year before. He would eventually become Middlesbrough manager in 1944, with Peter McWilliam making the journey in the opposite direction to become chief scout at Highbury.

George Camsell was one of only four people to give Middlesbrough Football Club over 30 years of service as player and then later, despite the cloud of Woodbine smoke that followed him everywhere, as a trainer. The other three men were Charlie Cole, Micky Fenton and Harold Shepherdson.

But we were talking about David Jack…

David Jack

Manager (1944–1952).

Just recently it was made clear that Darren, son of Sir Alex Ferguson, had inherited more than a few of his illustrious father's managerial gifts when he started to enjoy a successful time as manager of Peterborough United, and it made you think about other fathers and sons who took on the burden of football management. Brian and Nigel Clough sprang immediately to mind, but there was another rather more distant dynasty.

Bob Jack was a player for Plymouth Argyle before he became manager in 1910. He was there for 28 seasons and in 1919 gave a playing debut to his son, David Bone Nightingale Jack, who went on to score 11 goals in 48 appearances. But David was about to be elevated to a more auspicious stage. In 1920, he moved to Bolton Wanderers, a club his father had also played for, where David was about to make a name for himself. The 1923 FA Cup Final between Bolton and West Ham was the first at Wembley Stadium and, after only two minutes, David Jack secured his place in history by heading the first goal in a 2–0 victory. Jack repeated his success in 1926, scoring the only goal in a Cup Final win over Man City. And then, in 1928, history came calling again.

David Jack of Arsenal and as Boro manager.

David Jack scores the first Wembley Cup Final goal in 1923.

Bob Jack, father of David.

When Arsenal wanted a replacement for striker Charles Buchan, Jack was the obvious choice. The game's first transfer fee of over £10,000 doubling the previous record secured his services, and he remained a regular in the team through to the early 1930s, becoming along the way the first player to win the FA Cup with two different clubs.

After retiring from playing, he returned as manager to another of his father's old teams, Southend United, employing the old boy on a part-time basis as one of his scouts until 1940 when the mighty Boro came calling. David Jack was in charge at Ayresome until 1952, and if he never quite achieved the success that team probably deserved, he would never be forgotten either.

Chapter Eight
The 1950s

Wilf Mannion

(1936–1954) 369 appearances.

If you have ever seen the Incredible Hulk throwing the massed ranks of the United States militia around as though they were rag-dolls, then you probably have some idea of how First Division defences felt in the 1950s when they came up against Nat Lofthouse. So, it is all the more surprising that when he was selected for his first international duty abroad, it was felt that the legendary Bolton Wanderers centre-forward might need someone to make sure he was properly settled into the team hotel. Apparently Frankenstein's monster was out

Wilf Mannion and Nat Lofthouse.

of town, so the England coach, Walter Winterbottom, selected instead none other than Boro's own Wilf Mannion. Quite what Wilf's duties entailed beyond making sure the big man was safely tucked in for the night with a steaming mug of cocoa, it is difficult to imagine. Erring on the safe side, he left well alone. Perhaps Nat caught a fleeting glimpse of his diminutive minder every now and then, pretty much getting on with his own business, but that was more or less it. Except for where it really counted, out on the pitch.

Lofthouse achieved greatness, no less than Mannion himself. And, possibly, he remembered those early days of his own England career when he later talked of Wilf in the same breath as another global football icon:

'When I watched Pelé,' he said, 'I thought of Wilf. What's more, great though Pelé is, I am proud to think I played with as great a player…perhaps even greater.'

Wilf was at his peak during the 1950–51 season. It was a high-scoring period that included such scorelines as: Middlesbrough 8 Huddersfield 0, Middlesbrough 4 Wolves 3, Middlesbrough 4 Blackpool 3 and (to show you cannot have it all your own way, all the time) Derby County 6 Middlesbrough 0. A typical game of the time was on 9 December 1950 when Wilf scored twice in a 7–3 festival of goals against Charlton Athletic.

The Golden Boy taps the ball in after a goalmouth scramble.

Born in the year the club was founded and a player in the first Football League game, Bob Wanless was a life-long supporter of Middlesbrough FC.

Goodbye to Bob Wanless

Bob was as old as the club itself and united the generations. Born in 1876, he played in Boro's first League game in 1899, scored a vital goal or two, and then he took his seat in the stands. He was still there after two World Wars, watching each home game at Ayresome Park throughout the 1950s, a witness to all the great players who trod the turf, seeing so many of them come and go. Bob Wanless died in July 1963.

Brian Clough

(1955–61) 222 appearances.

The start of any football season is a magical time, when all things seem possible. But, as those early, sun-dappled days pass by, the real hard grind sets in. This was never more so than in the 1950s when, by Christmas time, many pitches had turned into mud-baths.

On 12 December 1959, on a misty afternoon in the Potteries, Middlesbrough FC beat Stoke City 5–2, the same score as their previous victory at Stoke's Victoria Ground in March 1956. This time the goals came from Eddie Holliday, Billy Day and a young Brian Clough. He is pictured close to the sludge-engulfed penalty spot, hooking the ball over the Stoke defender's head for one goal of the hat-trick he scored that day.

There are few nowadays who would regard the great man as anything but unique, but at the time he made his debut on 17 September 1955 in a home draw against Barnsley (no, he did not score, Arthur Fitzsimons did the honours), he was being welcomed as 'a second Camsell.' Which was fitting in a way since he was actually spotted by George Camsell himself, playing for Billingham Synthonia.

Even in those early days of his career Brian Howard Clough, only 19 at the time, had a somewhat forthright way of expressing himself, as in his opinion of Bob Dennison the manager who gave him his debut ahead of more experienced names such as Charlie Wayman and Ken McPherson:

'...hopeless – couldn't have spotted a diamond in a diamond mine.'

Opposite: Close to the sludge-engulfed penalty spot, he hooks the ball over the Stoke defender's head for one goal of the hat-trick he scored that day.

Chapter Nine
The 1960s

Tavistock Street

Shortly afterwards, on 7 October 1961 if I am going to be exact, for a home game in the Second Division against Liverpool, who would be promoted that season and never look back, I was taken to my first-ever match by my dad and my grandad.

The latter lived, as I briefly mentioned before, in Tavistock Street, just by the back of the South Stand at Ayresome, and I had been fascinated for years by his strange behaviour every Saturday. It would invariably go like this: he would set off all wrapped up, possibly with a flask of something hot, all cheerful and a friend, if not to the world, then at least to all those like-minded fellows whose procession he joined towards the football ground, where the faint oompah of the brass band that would have been marching up and down the pitch could be heard drifting through the heavy tobacco smoke-laden air.

Then, 90 minutes or so later, he would return all bad tempered and cursing all and sundry as grandma sat by the radio and pencilled in the other full-time results for him to check against his football pools, or for him just to have a good old moan about.

'What a load of rubbish!' he would declare. 'That's the last time I'm ever going there!'

Then a couple of weeks would pass and another home match would come round. The little house would rumble and echo with the footsteps on the cobbles outside of people going to the game, and grandad would get restless. Then he would disappear and swiftly return all muffled in his hat and coat.

'Alright!' he would say. 'I'm going to give them one more chance!'

Well, we beat Liverpool 2–0 that day and, for however brief a period, all was well with the world. Except I am sure I could overhear him muttering to himself 'Ye gods, did you see them this afternoon? There's not one of them knows how to trap a ball.'

I kept my head down and got on with my beans on toast.

Newcastle United v Middlesbrough

(Boxing Day 1961) League Division Two.

My next emotional investment in Middlesbrough Football Club came later that same season. It was the Boxing Day derby against Newcastle United at St James' Park. Not that we were at the game on this particular occasion. But

Ray Yeoman, Arthur Kaye and Ron Waldock all featured for Boro in the 1961–62 season.

(in those days before Teletext or Sky Sports *Soccer Special*) we were waiting for the final results to come up on BBC *Grandstand's* clattering old teleprinter. If you were in Middlesbrough town and the Boro were away you could keep up with how they were doing by looking in Forshaws the Tobacconist's window, where the kindly proprietor kept scribbling the latest scores on a piece of card.

At last the flickering grey light of the television started to illuminate the football results. We waited an age for the only score that really mattered until, at last, it started to come through: Newcastle 3 (my heart sank, fearing the worst)…Middlesbrough…4! I can still remember the feeling of elation. The

Newcastle match programme of the day had been certain the game would be a thriller, in fact going so far as to state: 'Whenever United and Middlesbrough are in opposition a grand game with thrills galore and excitement in abundance is generally the outcome.' Well, they certainly got that bit right.

To make things even better, Boro met Newcastle again in a game that should have been just a few days later on 30 December but was postponed to 7 March 1962, and they completed the double by beating them 3–0.

Alan Peacock

(1955–64) 238 appearances.

The picture shows Alan Peacock going to ground as he hooks the ball into the Newcastle net on that memorable Boxing Day in 1961. Ray Yeoman and Bill Harris (who scored the other three) look on. Alan was in his first full season since his demob from the army and well on his way to becoming one of my first Boro heroes.

Alan Peacock scoring the first of four goals on that memorable day against Newcastle.

Cyril Knowles

(1962–64) 39 appearances.

You cannot blame Jimmy Hill for everything. On 12 April 1963 Middlesbrough started a pretty gruelling set of fixtures. They faced Derby County at home and won 5–1. Then away the very next day to Rotherham, where they lost 4–1. After a whole day of rest they were then away to Derby again on 15 April and drew 3–3 in a match that marked the debut of a young full-back. Claiming the position

Nice one, Cyril.

that the England international Mick McNeil would soon relinquish when he moved to Ipswich, Cyril Knowles made 39 appearances until the end of the 1963–64 season when 'Glory, Glory' days were waiting. Sold to Tottenham Hotspur, he won FA Cup, League Cup and UEFA Cup medals.

Through no fault of his own, he even embellished his reputation as the focus of a pop song, *Nice One, Cyril*. Somehow I got it into my head that TV pundit, Jimmy Hill, wrote this choral triumph. I even used to inform certain Doubting Thomases that such was the case. Unfortunately (for me), I now discover that I have been doing a certain J. Spiro a disservice. For the rhyme turns out to be entirely his responsibility. Jimmy Hill does not get off the hook quite so easily, however, as he did write the lyrics for *Good Old Arsenal*. And that, of course, puts Jimmy right back in the ranks of dubious football song writers.

Eddie Connachan

(1963–1966) 105 appearances.

As an ex-goalkeeper myself (in the York and District Railway League Division Five), I have always had a special affection for the men who wore the green jersey, and this man was no exception. Edward Devlin Connachan made his goalkeeping name with Dalkeith Thistle and Dunfermline Athletic.

In 1961, he was generally regarded as having defied Celtic pretty much single-handedly in the Scottish Cup Final and replay, being chaired off the pitch by victorious teammates after Dunfermline won 2–0. Billy McNeill of Celtic regarded the performance as 'superhuman.' Not forgetting that Eddie had worked two coalmine shifts in between the games. In August 1963, £5,500 brought him to Middlesbrough. At the time, a number of solutions to regular 'keeper Bob Appleby's persistent injury problems had been looked for. Esmond Million, Morris Emmerson and Arthur Lightening (who, in a less-than-auspicious debut, conceded six on 29 August 1962, away to Newcastle) had all been tried, along with Des McPartland, who outlasted all the others.

But Eddie made the position his own for two seasons, 1963–64 and 1964–65. He was strong and fearless, and my dad and I thought he was a worthy inheritor of the Appleby mantle, passed on since the late 1940s by Ugolini and then Taylor. In the picture, he is making sure the ball is not going anywhere in a game from 12 October 1963, a 3–1 win over Portsmouth at Ayresome Park. And was that low, westering sun not always a curse for the bedazzled North Terrace?

Ultimately, 1966 saw Eddie Connachan's last appearance for the team and, while Bob Appleby made a brief return and Des McPartland did sterling work, a new legend was waiting in the wings. His name was Willie Whigham.

Eddie Connachan making sure the ball is not going anywhere it should not.

Willie Whigham
(1966–72) 214 appearances.
Part One.

William Murdoch Morrison Whigham, after signing from Falkirk, made his debut as Middlesbrough goalkeeper on 8 October 1966, away to Watford. Although the team lost 2–0 that day, it was the start of a sometimes controversial period when he saw off the challenge of McPartland, vied with Maurice Short and won the right to be regarded as the Middlesbrough number one. It was also an unforgettable season.

In the previous campaign, proving what is so often the case that great players do not necessarily make great managers, Raich Carter's Middlesbrough had been relegated. Finding itself in the Third Division for the first time in its history with Stan Anderson now in charge, the club was finding life in the lower levels far from easy. At the time that Willie took over in goal, Boro had just gone down 5–1 to Gillingham, with McPartland the unfortunate 'keeper on the wrong end of a battering. The result sent Middlesbrough Football Club to second from bottom of Division Three.

But with Willie in goal and John O'Rourke, John Hickton and Arthur Horsfield hitting the net on an increasingly regular basis, things really started to turn around.

Willie Whigham.

At Christmas time a 4–0 win over Colchester, followed by 3–0 and 4–0 victories against Darlington home and away, meant the top part of the League table was no longer quite such a distant country. All the more so as a strong finish to the season inspired another dream of promotion.

Willie kept a clean sheet as Torquay were seen off 4–0, then a 1–1 draw at Brighton meant that, with two home games left against Peterborough and Oxford United respectively, Boro would be promoted if they won both. Ayresome Park was packed with 32,000 spectators for the Peterborough game and a 2–1 triumph, but no one could quite have anticipated anything like what happened next. A crowd of 40,000 people witnessed Boro win 4–1 to finish the season in second place in the division – good enough to be promoted. In Willie Whigham's own words:

'We knew we would beat Oxford. It was party time. The atmosphere that night was unbelievable. I've never known anything like it. There were 40,000 there and they invaded the pitch every time we scored. John O'Rourke knocked the goals in. He was some boy.'

Arthur Horsfield.

Arthur Horsfield
(1963–69) 121 appearances.

My best memory of Arthur Horsfield is a blistering shot that he scored with, in front of the Holgate End, against Crystal Palace on 20 August 1968, in a 4–0 triumph. Arthur scored twice, with Johnny Crossan and Ray Lugg getting the other two goals (it was also the game that had Middlesbrough skipper Gordon Jones asking the referee to tell the Palace team to switch their red shorts for white ones to avoid clashing with the Boro shirts. The ref duly sent them back to the changing room).

Gordon Jones *(1961–73) 527 appearances.*

& Johnny Crossan *(1967–70) 61 appearances.*

Middlesbrough captain Gordon Jones looks on as Johnny Crossan prepares to take the free-kick that led to him scoring the club's winning goal in a 1–0 victory over Portsmouth at Ayresome Park on 8 March 1969. If you look carefully, you might see, just beyond Jones's shoulder, a young fellow in the crowd, enjoying the rare luxury of watching the game from a seat in the North Stand, Kodak instamatic camera poised at the ready, about to record the moment for posterity (I was 17 at the time, in the days when beer and girls still took a back seat to watching the mighty Boro). Gordon Jones, of course, is a legendary Middlesbrough captain, with a modern-day record number of full-back appearances and if not for Ray Wilson's form in those days could quite easily have been in the England World Cup-winning side.

Johnny Crossan is probably less well remembered, but there are not many insomniac players, at one time banned for life from the English game, who went on to achieve his kind of success. The ban was for an alleged illegal payment made to him as an amateur with Coleraine in the Irish League. Undeterred, he did well enough for himself in Holland with Sparta Rotterdam and in Belgium, in the European Cup, with Standard Liege. In 1962 the ban was lifted and he signed for Sunderland, winning promotion with them in 1964. In 1965 he signed for Manchester City and was their captain when they were promoted to Division One. He was a Northern Ireland international when Middlesbrough signed him from City in 1967, for what was then a record fee of £35,000.

Alex Smith
(1965–1972) 135 appearances.
Present-day kit man.

My favourite Bristol City moment was on 13 September 1969. It was almost half-time at Ayresome Park, and Derrick Downing had put Boro 1–0 up in the

Johnny Crossan and
Gordon Jones.

third minute. Unfortunately, though, we were struggling to really put the game out of reach. But, 'cometh the hour cometh the man'. Alex Smith actually made his Boro debut against City on 5 March 1966 but had not become a regular until late in the 1967–68 season. He was a full-back who went on to make 131 League and Cup appearances, but he only ever scored one goal, and this was it.

Alex had been battered by a City player and, as I remember it, was actually unconscious on the pitch receiving treatment for quite some time. Head swathed in bloody bandages, he was eventually able to get back to his feet.

With determination etched in every sinew, he proceeded to take the subsequent free-kick himself. It might just be the way I remember it, but in my imagination it was not far from the halfway line when he came thundering through the mud and belted the ball with all his strength. It went crashing into the net at the Holgate End and was as emphatic a response to being fouled as I think I have ever seen.

We eventually won the game 2–0, with Alex enduring the second half, his head still wrapped around with bandages. It prompted one of those renowned humorists on the South Terrace to shout out 'Come on, Tonto!', which might have seemed a bit on the disrespectful side. Then again, you could say it was an appropriate description for a hero, shrugging off his own injuries, who had just come charging to the rescue. For Alex then: 'Hi-yo, Silver, Away!'

The *Lone Ranger* had been on TV since the 1950s and inspired the terrace shout of 'Come on, Tonto!'

Charlton v Middlesbrough

League Division Two (5 April 1968).

Stan Anderson nearly led Middlesbrough to the Promised Land. That they ultimately fell short should not detract from the fact that he took a team that was a struggling Third Division outfit and turned it into a genuine contender for promotion to the highest level. Every season we believed it was going to be our year, and every season, well, it never quite turned out to be. Until such a time as Stan felt he had done as much as he could do, and it was possibly time to let someone else have a go. He never got closer than the 1968–69 season.

All through the season the club vied with Crystal Palace and Charlton, along with challenges from Cardiff City and Huddersfield, for the second promotion spot behind runaway leaders, Brian Clough's Derby County. By the time that the vital Easter period came around, with games running out, Middlesbrough were still in the race but had started to slip with a 3–0 defeat at Carlisle and a 1–1 draw with Blackburn Rovers (albeit sandwiched around a memorable 5–3 victory over Hull City). The club's challenge was still hanging by a thread, but the fixture list did not help at all. Coming up next was a home game against Cardiff then, over Easter, on successive days, away to Crystal Palace and then Charlton – the three teams that were Middlesbrough's closest rivals.

The match against Cardiff was the first and last game I ever took my mother to. I am not saying it was her fault that we only drew 0–0, but good and bad luck is a delicately balanced thing and you should not factor too many new elements into the equation. Besides, it meant I could not swear when things were going wrong. All was not lost though. If the team could win the two away games over Easter, it was still on.

4 April 1968: Crystal Palace 0–0 Middlesbrough. OK, but at least it was not a defeat. And the *Daily Mail* report said that Middlesbrough will long be remembered, not so much for the quality of their play, but for the sporting way

A typical hard-fought home win in November 1968. Boro 2 Blackburn Rovers 0. Rovers player John Coddington scored an own-goal for Boro just a short time before joining the Ayresome coaching staff.

they quickly fetched the ball and returned it to the opposition whenever it went out of play.

Now it was a question of going to Charlton Athletic and getting a positive result. Middlesbrough had triumphed in that arena before, or at least come away intact in the FA Cup back on 25 January 1930 when, after a 0–0 draw at the Valley, followed by another 1–1 draw at Ayresome Park, Boro won the second replay 1–0 at Maine Road, Manchester. The Addicks themselves had been formed in 1905, when their nickname was derived from the haddock nailed to a board that a local fishmonger used to bring to home games. This was a somewhat smelly precursor to the modern-day form of mascot, so nobly represented by Middlesbrough's own beloved Roary the Lion.

By the way, Charlton's first-ever manager was the mysterious Walter Rayner, who is conspicuous by his absence in team photographs of the period. And, while one cannot help but feel a twinge of pride that a namesake played his part in the early days of the great game, there is perhaps a sense of disappointment that he was ultimately sacked in 1925 for financial irregularities. Though he went on to manage Wigan Borough, he was subsequently banned for life from the game in 1926, and

Opposite: Big John Hickton in action on 1 February 1969. Promotion was still on when the game at Burnden Park, played in pouring rain, finished goalless. Dickie Rooks, a man who could head a ball further than most could kick it, is standing by.

Below: Stan Webb in white tries to knock the ball past Charlton's Ray Crawford, while the Holgate End's favourite visiting goalkeeper, Charlie Wright, looks on.

nothing more is known about him, except that 'he possibly emigrated to the United States.' – probably no relation.

Unfortunately, Charlton Athletic saw off Middlesbrough's faint hopes of promotion that Easter time in 1968, despite the efforts of one of the club's lesser-known heroes, Stan Webb (who had replaced Arthur Horsfield at centre-forward that season).

That was it for yet another season. A goalless draw with Norwich, a 3–2 home defeat to relegated Bury (significant for the debut that day of young Willie Maddren who, as a forward, scored one of the consolation goals) and a final defeat, 3–1 to Birmingham left us to finish up at fourth place in the League table. Derby and Crystal Palace were promoted.

Hugh McIlmoyle saw off the not inconsiderable challenge of ex-Sunderland hard man, Charlie Hurley, to score.

Willie Whigham
(1966–72) 214 appearances.
Part Two.

Willie had held onto the 'keeper's role at the higher level, though he did court controversy at times. At the beginning of the 1969–70 season, for instance, it seemed as though he had fallen out with the club to such an extent that he handed Maurice Short his place in the team. Whatever overtures were made to Willie, they failed, and from August through to October his tall, gangly figure was missed by the Ayresome Park regulars. Then, somehow, peace was brokered, or so it seemed at least according to the local press. Willie would return to the fray for the next day's game at home to Bolton Wanderers (Boro's first-ever appearance on *Match of the Day*, 11 October 1969, albeit on the then regional section of the programme).

It was a grey freezing afternoon at Ayresome, and the terraces, if not completely packed, were still agog awaiting the reappearance of the legendary goalkeeper. The team came out, red shirt following red shirt into the drizzling rain but no sign of the eagerly anticipated man in green.

'Oh, God,' someone said. 'He's not turned up!'

And it certainly looked that way as necks craned to get a better view down that narrow dimly lit players tunnel. The Bolton team came out, all present and correct, while the Middlesbrough team continued the pre-match formalities without a goalkeeper in sight. Then the discontented murmur that was spreading through the crowd suddenly changed in tone to a few muted uncertain cheers that quickly turned into a full-throated roar of recognition. Because a tall, rangy figure had loped out of the players' tunnel to light up the murky afternoon. Willy Whigham was back in our midst, and the stadium rose to him. Whatever last-minute negotiations might or might not have been going on, or whether he just played the moment for all its dramatic worth, or possibly just had to attend to some private but irresistible function, he was back and that was all that mattered.

Suitably inspired, the team went on to set about Bolton Wanderers to win comfortably, 4–0. John Hickton scored twice and Hugh McIlmoyle saw off the not inconsiderable challenge of ex-Sunderland hard man, Charlie Hurley to score two more. And how do I know all this? Because I was there, shivering to death on the South Terrace wondering if I would ever be able to feel my feet again.

Having reclaimed his place in the Middlesbrough goal and seemingly having settled his differences with the club, Willie never missed a game as the 1970–71 season came and went. He played 42 times in the League, three in the FA Cup – including a 2–1 replay victory over Manchester

Willie Whigham was brave and athletic in an angular, disjointed kind of way.

United, which we will get to in good time – and two in the League Cup. He was a brave, athletic 'keeper in an angular, disjointed kind of way and a mainstay in the team.

I once heard an irate supporter, and we have had one or two of those in our time, shout from the North Terrace 'Put that fag out, Whigham!' And there remains, as part of his legend, the apocryphal stories of him 'borrowing' cigarettes from fans if the game was not keeping the great man busy enough. To be fair, in those days that kind of thing was not entirely unknown. Charlie Wright, then of Charlton, lit up his visits to Ayresome Park by chatting with supporters as he sat on the wall behind the goal, fortifying himself with an inhalation or two of the dreaded weed. Charlie always said that Ayresome was one of his favourite grounds because of the friendly reception he always got from the fans, thereby establishing himself as a fellow of rare good taste.

In addition, of course, we have already witnessed Jeremiah Dawkings back in the 1800s establishing the tradition of tobacco-saturated goalkeepers. But, in Willie's case, the accusations are unjust. My personal belief is that it was a nasal inhaler that he was using to open up his airways and keep him ready for battle.

There he is, brave as ever, hurling himself at the feet of Eddie McCreadie of Chelsea, in a League Cup game at Stamford Bridge on 7 October 1970, while Boro skipper Gordon Jones looks on. Three goals down at half-time, Boro fought back, scoring twice in the last minute to almost snatch a draw.

Big John Hickton got one and the other was a rare goal from Jones himself. Boro had put those grim Third Division days behind them and were starting to make an impression. Or, as Sir Matt Busby said after they beat Manchester United that same season, 'What on earth are Middlesbrough doing in the Second Division?'

We had better see what he was talking about. But just before we do, it would be wrong not to mention another great goalkeeper who took over from Willie in 1971 and dominated the position for over a decade to come. He saw off pretenders to his throne like Pat Cuff and James Stewart along the way, until 1983 when Kelham O'Hanlon took over, to be followed in his turn by the great Steve Pears. Hats off, then, to Jim Platt too.

Arnold Hills as a young man...

...and, after a lifetime of clean living, still going strong as old age settled upon him.

Chapter Ten
The 1970s

Middlesbrough v West Ham United
(January 3 1970) FA Cup Third Round.

It was the great West Ham United team, including the World Cup-winning trio of Bobby Moore, Geoff Hurst and Martin Peters, along with the emerging talents of Trevor Brooking, against a Middlesbrough team that at that time was in the Second Division and managed by Stan Anderson. The FA Cup of 1970 brought both clubs together.

It was a golden age for West Ham United and possibly only Manchester United could rival them in regard to the sheer crowd-pulling potential of the players they boasted. Historically, they were not quite as venerable an old club as Middlesbrough. Indeed, when Boro were winning the FA Amateur Cup for the first time in 1895, West Ham were only just a twinkle in the eye of a certain David Taylor and his employer Mister Arnold Hills of the Thames Ironworks. As a young man, Arnold had played football for Harrow, Oxford University, even got a game for Old Harrovians and once for England. And when we say 'football' in the Harrow context, we mean a somewhat primitive ancestor of the modern game. He was of a generation of players such as Lord Kinnaird of Wanderers and Old Etonians, whose doting mother, concerned about the rough game her son played and worrying that he would come home with a broken leg, confided her fears to her butler and was reassured when he replied 'Don't worry ma'am, it won't be his own.'

Arnold Hills kept himself fit. He was a teetotaller and a committed vegetarian, and old age settled gracefully upon him. So, in the summer of 1865, when David Taylor, his foreman (and football referee), at Thames Ironworks suggested they form a football team, the benevolent old philanthropist was all for it. All for anything, in fact, that would keep the young fellows healthy.

It would be five more years before Thames Ironworks Football Club changed their name to West Ham United, but they retained their heritage in the nicknames, 'The Irons' or 'The Hammers.' And then, some years later (in 1965 to be

precise), Derrick Downing signed for Middlesbrough. His date with destiny
and West Ham United was 3 January 1970.

It was a great Cup tie. Boro took the lead in front of a packed house in the
first-half through Hugh McIlmoyle. Then, in the second half, Clyde Best scored
for West Ham. There were only five minutes to go when the First Division team
were subjected to the same doom that Ayresome Park regulars were used to
seeing inflicted on admittedly lesser opposition.

Pitching in headfirst, where weaker men were afraid to stick their boots, Derrick Downing got the winner with a diving header. He is sprawled over the Hammers 'keeper, while Boro captain Gordon Jones salutes the goal in the background.

I am sure that it is perfectly correct that the late Bobby Moore is remembered as a gentleman of the game; however, as a youngster on the North Terrace close to the players tunnel that day, I shall never forget the disillusionment of seeing Moore constantly arguing with the referee. Then he encapsulated a performance of unparalleled petulance by sarcastically applauding the referee as he left the pitch, for 'losing West Ham the game.' So, that was the England captain, I thought. Maybe so, and good luck to him. But you never saw Gordon Jones carrying on like that.

That was a good season in the FA Cup. Next up was another thriller against York City that Middlesbrough won 4–1 and then a nail-biting 2–1 triumph over Carlisle United. All part of a journey that was leading to the sixth round and a date with giants.

Surrounded by West Ham's legendary players, Derek Downing got the winner with a diving header.

Middlesbrough v Manchester United

(21 February 1970) FA Cup Sixth Round.

In that winter of 1970 it was freezing cold as we trudged up Green Lane in the snow and ice to join the queue for tickets that stretched from the Ayresome Park ticket office, past the General Hospital, all the way down Roman Road. This was because Stan Anderson's Boro, a Second Division side of unrealised potential, had been drawn at home in the FA Cup to the team that everybody wanted to see, the recent European Champions, Manchester United. George Best wove through the Boro half-back line of George Smith, Bill Gates and Frank Spraggon, with the kind of incomparable magic that would light up the bleakest of mid-winters. On 21 February 1970 it was part of the beginning of a three-season sequence, where, in one competition or another, Boro always came up against the Red Devils. In 1969–70, we had already gone out of the League Cup to a David Sadler goal at Old Trafford when we drew in the FA Cup, 1–1 at home, losing the replay 2–1.

We had the same glacial ticket vigil to endure the next season in January 1971, to see Boro actually beat the same illustrious opponents 2–1 after a goalless draw at Old Trafford. And then again in February 1972, to witness another Ayresome replay. It was the time of the miners' strike, and the game was played on a Tuesday afternoon because of the threat of evening power cuts. In fact the latter circumstance still impacted on the game, enforcing one of the rare occasions when the Boro's signature tune, the ironically named *The Power Game*, was not played as the team took to the field. Nobby Stiles captained Middlesbrough against his old team and received a memorable ovation from everyone in the ground as he shook hands with Bobby Charlton before the game. The workplaces, schools and colleges of Teesside were strangely deserted that grey afternoon, and the atmosphere generated by the crowd was enough to create its own electricity. At least until Boro went behind in the first half, then crumbled a bit as things progressed, eventually going down 3–0.

Nobby Stiles

(1971–73) 69 appearances.

Nobby Stiles played 392 times for his childhood heroes, Manchester United, including a night of glory in the 1968 European Cup Final victory over Benfica, before transferring to Boro in 1971. If his ball-winning skills were on the wane, there was still enough about the tenacious little devil for him to replace Gordon Jones as team captain at Ayresome Park. Then, because football does things like this, as we have just seen, only months after leaving Old Trafford he was on his way back, leading Boro out in that fifth round FA Cup tie on 26 February 1972. Despite the 53,000 crowd welcoming him home as one of their own, he was faithful to his new team in a determined performance that earned a goalless draw and a replay at Ayresome. This, as we have just seen, did not really go all that well.

Meanwhile, north of the border, a dashing centre-forward by the name of Alex Ferguson had just celebrated the birth of his twin sons before getting back to the serious business of banging the goals in for Falkirk. A playing career that had started at Queens Park, taking in the likes of St Johnstone, Dunfermline and Rangers, would include one more transfer to Ayr United before it drew to a close. But, it had already occurred to young Ferguson that there was an aptitude in him for that managerial lark. Consequently, by 1974, in that capacity, he was on his way via East Stirling, St Mirren, and Aberdeen to Manchester United.

As if it was not enough to achieve success on the pitch with the awesome team he fashioned, he had an eye on the future too, with the youngsters whose responsibility it would be to sustain it. Names like Beckham, Giggs, and Scholes were appearing on the team sheet for the juniors, and all they needed was a guiding hand. So, Alex Ferguson brought an old warhorse home and appointed Nobby Stiles as his youth-team coach.

Opposite: 53,000 people welcomed Nobby Stiles as one of their own, while north of the border; Alex Ferguson was turning out for Falkirk.

Manchester United v Middlesbrough
(8 October 1973)

After lasting the whole 1972–73 season without drawing Manchester United in either of the Cups, when the next year got underway the inevitable happened yet again. From 1969 through the early 1970s, whenever the FA Cup came around, Middlesbrough always seemed to get drawn against Manchester United. In fact, as we have already seen, in the 1969–70 season both FA and League Cups meant awe-inspiring trips to Old Trafford. It was only in 1968 that United had been European Champions, and all their great stars, including Denis Law who had missed out on glory in Europe due to injury, were still there, ready, willing and more than able to torment us.

It was my first trip to Old Trafford for the League Cup tie to see one of those European heroes, David Sadler, score the only goal of the game at the Stretford End. A 1–0 defeat should not have seemed so bad at the home of legends, but there was a nagging feeling that Boro had been just a little bit unlucky. We were getting used to heroic defeats in those days. That sense of not quite being able to make it was one of the frustrations of Stan Anderson's Middlesbrough team. The next two seasons followed a familiar pattern. Always drawn away, Middlesbrough invariably held out for a hard-fought draw. In 1970–71, McIllmoyle and Downing goals (repeating their heroics of the previous season against West Ham United), actually secured a rare replay victory, 2–1, at Ayresome Park. But the general rule was that United eventually took away the spoils.

Old Trafford itself was not an especially happy hunting ground. Those with exceptionally long memories might recall Middlesbrough's unbeaten run there from 1911 to 1922, but even supporters of a slightly more recent vintage had to go all the way back to 14 January 1933 for the last Boro victory there, 4–1 in the FA Cup. So, in 1973, when the League Cup draw was made, the inevitable happened: 8 October, Manchester United versus Middlesbrough, at Old Trafford. But times were changing, and United were now a team in decline. And, in Big Jack Charlton's first season in charge, Middlesbrough Football Club was on the rise. That 'not quite good enough' tag was about to be thrown away for at least the foreseeable future. As though to exemplify all that, the Old Trafford hoodoo was beaten at last. Boro went there and won 1–0.

'Middlesbrough were simply superb, superbly simple,' enthused the local media, waxing lyrical, and even the *Daily Mirror*, representing the national press, agreed: 'Certainly there was only one team of First Division class out there – and it wasn't Manchester United.'

Alan Foggon charged through the middle, taking no prisoners, and Willie Morgan and George Graham pursued in vain, though credit should also go to Malcolm Smith who scored the winning goal. It was a game in which it really started to look as though Boro could hold their own at a higher level and rid

Alan Foggon charged through the middle, taking
no prisoners, and Willie Morgan and George
Graham pursued in vain.

themselves of the curse of gallant failure. The Second Division Championship was subsequently won by a record margin, while United endured an unhappier time. The champions of just six years earlier were relegated that season, although it should be said that they did not exactly disappear without trace. They were soon on their way back, and the rest, of course, is history.

Bobby Murdoch, the Lisbon Lion.

As for Middlesbrough, what had really made the difference? Jack Charlton had essentially the same players at his disposal as Stan Anderson had before him. Except for one notable addition…

Bobby Murdoch

(1973–76) 113 appearances.

There were some who had enjoyed European football before they came to Middlesbrough, some who went on to it after they left. Not too many who endured it during their time at Ayresome Park, unless you count the Anglo-Italian Cup. And then there was a Lisbon Lion.

Bobby Murdoch had been a part of the Celtic team that were the first British winners of the European Cup in 1967, but when he came to Middlesbrough in 1973 he might have appeared to be somewhat less than the super-fit athlete of the modern game. Appearances can be deceptive, however, and he became a vital part of Jack Charlton's promotion winners. All in all, he made 125 appearances, helping to establish the club in the top division, disdaining to chase a ball bobbling more than two yards ahead of him but delivering it impeccably to its target if he found it at his feet. On 13 January 1976 the old lion could still roar. He played at Ayresome Park in the League Cup semi-final against Manchester City and described the atmosphere as 'making the hairs on the back of your neck stand up.' High praise for the Boro faithful from a man who had played in Old Firm derbies and European Cup Finals.

Middlesbrough v Chelsea

League Division One (7 September 1974-75).

As the 1974–75 season kicked-off, Jack Charlton's Middlesbrough team were back in the First Division after an absence of 20 years. On 7 September, despite good away victories at Birmingham and Carlisle, they were still looking for their first home win.

Chelsea were the visitors, and Boro took the lead in the first half. Willie Maddren, despite having made his debut as a striker (against Bury, 12 April 1969), had by now matured into one of the great defenders, not that it stopped him still putting the ball into the net every once in a while. He did so on this occasion, saluting his goal while Middlesbrough captain and centre-half (what were they both doing so far up the pitch?) Stuart Boam and Brian Taylor join in the celebrations.

I was there, in the Holgate End, down by the corner flag. I heard the referee talking to Chelsea player Charlie Cooke, who was trying to waste time before taking a corner.

'Come on, Charlie,' he said. 'Get on with it.'

Willie Maddren salutes
his goal against
Chelsea.

And I remember thinking, what chance do the Boro have if the ref is on first-name terms with the opposition? The game ended 1–1, but the first home win of that season was not entirely elusive and came two weeks later, 3–0 against Manchester City. It was a season that saw the club as high as second in the table at Christmas, and Bill Shankly, the Liverpool manager no less, tipped Middlesbrough as a good outside bet for the title (they finished seventh, the tradition of heroic failure not quite shaken off).

In 1952 Shankly had almost become Middlesbrough manager after David Jack and before Walter Rowley took over, with Harold Shepherdson as his assistant. Somewhere along the line negotiations broke down, but it might have been interesting.

Arsenal v Middlesbrough

(30 November 1974)

OK, Middlesbrough lost the game 2–0, but it does show that, although newly promoted, they were more than holding their own at the top level. And it was still a memorable season. There were away wins at, among others, Spurs (2–1 and 4–0 in the League Cup. 'Boring Boro' said the southern press), Liverpool 1–0 (League Cup again) and Chelsea 2–1.

Frank Spraggon and Willie Maddren challenging Arsenal's John Radford.

Of course there was also the away kit that Boro wore in those days. The blue-and-black striped shirt remains a personal favourite (though the light blue shorts never quite matched). In fact, my lucky matchday scarf is in those colours and from that era. In the days before extensive merchandising, it was knitted by my grandma, who was still living in the little house in Tavistock Street right outside Ayresome Park, though I believe she had given up charging people a penny a time for use of her ladder to get to the top of the South Stand. She was not going to games any more though. I only took her once, and that was on 12 October 1968 when Sheffield United were the visitors. Not content with just watching the action and quietly applauding Boro's 3–1 victory, she took it upon herself to start berating the Middlesbrough goalkeeper of the day, Willie Whigham.

'You're not as good as Ugolini!' she cried out.

'Bloody Hell, missus,' said a man in the crowd, turning round to stare at her. 'When were you last here?'

My memory might me playing me false here, but I have a sneaking suspicion I pinched the scarf from my brother, for whom it was originally intended, but it has served me well over the years.

Middlesbrough v Wycombe Wanderers
FA Cup third-round replay (7 January 1975).
On 4 January 1975 Middlesbrough were away to Wycombe Wanderers, a non-League team at that time, in the FA Cup third round. We made the arduous journey to Wycombe and gaped agog at the notorious slope of that old ground of theirs, Loakes Park. It really looked as if it would take an experienced mountaineer to get from one side of the pitch to the other. But, since Sir Edmund Hillary was not available, they decided they would play football on the ground instead.

We took our places on the terrace, in those days before crowd segregation, and listened to the Wycombe supporters as they watched the Boro players during the pre-match warm up. David 'Spike' Armstrong in particular caught their eye, and having marvelled at his skills one man turned to his friend and asked:

'What do you think our chances are then?'

'I reckon they'll beat us 8–0,' he replied.

'I'd settle for 5–0,' the other man concluded.

It did not happen quite like that. In fact, arguably, Wycombe deserved better than the 0–0 final score. We were more relieved than jubilant as the replay date, 7 January, quickly came around, underneath the floodlights of Ayresome Park. And the words of those Wycombe supporters proved prophetic, if not in terms of the scoreline, at least in their expressed

admiration of David Armstrong. With extra-time looming (a rare event in those days), Spike scored the winning penalty in the 89th minute of the game. But it had certainly been a close-run thing, and Wycombe Wanderers fully deserved the standing ovation the whole ground gave them as they left the pitch.

This was the game that tested to its utmost the theory my dad and I had. The Theory of the Lucky Cigarette. It was part of the family legend that every time we lit up, Middlesbrough scored, but on this occasion (and, to be honest, on many others), it failed us. As we coughed away our frustration, a decision of some magnitude was made. We both decided to give up smoking.

David Armstrong scoring the winner against Wycombe in the 89th minute while Alan Willey looks on.

David Mills sandwiched between Kenny Burns and the Birmingham goalkeeper.

Middlesbrough v Birmingham City

(26 August 1975)

It was a time when players had the sort of big hair that nowadays you would only see on the more flamboyant type of South American footballer. But in 1976 a flowing mane was no handicap to emerging domestic talent, nor was it any indication of the innate toughness or otherwise of First Division footballers.

The previous season, Middlesbrough had started the First Division campaign with a 3–0 victory at Birmingham City, completing the double with another 3–0 success at Ayresome Park in December, although the Blues gained some modicum of revenge by knocking Boro out of the FA Cup in the sixth round.

When 1975–76 came around they were looking to progress even further. Birmingham were visitors for the second home game of the season on 26 August. Two goals in two minutes won it. The first came from Big John Hickton and the second from David Mills. The latter is pictured fighting for the ball, sandwiched between the Birmingham 'keeper and Kenny Burns, golden locks ablaze in the late summer sunshine. If Mills never quite won the hearts of all the crowd, it was never for want of trying, and he remains an underestimated part of Ayresome folklore. A quality player. As was Kenny Burns who, two years later, was voted Footballer of the

Year when he had moved on to Nottingham Forest under the managerial magic wand of Boro old boy, Brian Clough.

And what about the progress that Middlesbrough Football Club had hoped for? Well, it was the season they won the Anglo-Scottish Cup.

Middlesbrough v Chelsea
(16 December 1978)

I knew someone once, Middlesbrough born and bred, who went to London for a long weekend. This person, who shall remain nameless, came home not only with a cockney accent but also proclaiming undying support for Chelsea Football Club. This was in the late 1970s when the Blues were comparative newcomers to the top division, having been promoted in 1977, a highlight in a period of struggle for the Stamford Bridge team.

John Bumstead scored a consolation for Chelsea, but the day belonged to Mark Proctor and the Boro team.

Terry Cochrane, another Boro scorer, alongside Peter Osgood who had opened the scoring for Chelsea on his second debut for the club.

Opposite: Micky Burns got four Boro goals, despite the presence of Ron 'Chopper' Harris.

This must have appealed to my born-again cockney friend, and he wasted no opportunity in telling us how much better Chelsea were than our own beloved Boro. He was looking forward immensely to their visit to Ayresome Park on 16 December 1978, when we would have the opportunity to see 'what a proper football team looked like.'

On top of everything else, this was to be the debut for the new Chelsea manager, Danny Blanchflower, still basking in clouds of glory from his immaculate playing career with Tottenham Hotspur. In addition, it was also to be the second Chelsea debut for yet another legend, the late, great Peter Osgood who had just returned from the United States. My friend was apoplectic with glee, and the rest of us huddled on the freezing cold terraces in some trepidation. It did not get much better when Osgood put Chelsea ahead early in the game. But then everything changed, and we all forgot about the cold.

While it is true that John Bumstead added a second for Chelsea, it was a mere consolation. In the meantime, Mark Proctor, Terry Cochrane, David Armstrong and Micky Burns, who hit the net four times, had won the game for John Neal's Boro. All the scorers from both sides are pictured (with the exception of 'Spike' Armstrong), along with the legendary Chelsea defender, Ron 'Chopper' Harris, holding off a challenge from Micky Burns.

The final score was 7–2, and the taunts were effectively stifled. In fact, we never heard a lot more from a certain quarter. My friend was not even able to enjoy a small measure of revenge when Chelsea beat Boro 2–1 later in the season at the Bridge, but nor did he have to suffer the subsequent heartbeak of their relegation. By this time his affections had long since wandered after a day out on Merseyside. You can probably guess the rest.

Chapter Eleven
The 1980s

David Shearer
(1977–83) 102 appearances.

So, when you hear the name 'Shearer' do you think of the hard, aggressive, immensely troublesome Newcastle United centre-forward of recent times, or does your mind drift back to 4 April 1978? That was the day that David Shearer made his Middlesbrough debut. Nowadays, scoring both goals in a 2–0 win over Chelsea in your first-ever game would be enough to elevate you to instant superstar status. And, as he got to grips with the 1980s, to follow it up with a last-minute winner against Liverpool and one goal in a 5–0 thrashing of Arsenal, plus a late equaliser a year later against the latter opposition again, this time at Highbury, you would think your place in the higher firmament of the game might be well and truly established.

Unfortunately, David never achieved the plaudits that would come his namesake's way when, just a few years later, Alan Shearer's career started to take off at Southampton. In that brief time, the game had started to evolve into the media-feeding monster that we have grown used to. And if David's achievements had been just a little later, you cannot help thinking that things might have been quite different.

Late goals were something of a speciality for David Shearer. Wolves (twice), Arsenal and Villa were all among the victims of that dramatic sting in the tail. So, in those all too brief early years of the 1980s, in difficult times, we have enough

Alan Shearer, immensely troublesome.

to thank David Shearer for. And, like his more famous namesake, he did eventually get to wear the famous black-and-white stripes. Of Grimsby, after his transfer in 1983. Oh, but the 1980s…there was a terrible time just around the corner.

David Shearer, a superstar before his time.

Bernie Slaven

(1985–1993) 356 appearances.

My brother and I were there. The home of Leeds United Football Club, Elland Road, 12 October 1985, to see a spindly young fellow called Bernie Slaven make his Middlesbrough debut.

Unfortunately, our tickets were in the Leeds end of the ground and, as the Boro lost that game 1–0, our 'try not to react if we score' resolve was never put to the test. Those were different days, and the team was struggling more than just a bit, and if we had known what was going on behind the scenes it would have broken our hearts. As it turned out, they were almost broken anyway as the club were relegated to Division Three at the end of the season, and there was worse

to come during the summer that lay ahead. Back in October, however, there was enough on view to suggest that our new striker might be a bit of alright.

In fact, he went on to score on his home debut against Bradford City a week later, setting himself on the road to achieving legendary status. Things would really improve for him in the season to come, but we had little idea then that just surviving to get to that point would be a nerve-wracking affair. Bruce Rioch would have taken over by then and, as unlikely as it seemed for a while, a whole new glorious chapter was about to begin. A club on the verge of going out of existence would rise from the ashes and win instant promotion back to Division Two. And then 1986–87 was going to be quite a season too, despite an inauspicious early setback or two that included a 3–1 away defeat to Crystal Palace. Bernie Slaven (pictured) scored the consolation goal that day. In fact it would soon be getting to the point where he could not stop scoring.

Missing out on automatic promotion to the top flight by the narrowest of margins, a recent innovation meant that there was a second chance – the dreaded Play-offs. One of my greatest Middlesbrough moments is of being on a packed South Terrace for the second leg against Bradford City, perfectly positioned to see Bernie score the first goal in a 2–0 win. At the Holgate End, of course. It was not just Bernie. There were heroes everywhere you looked in that young team. From Pears in goal to Laws and Glover and Cooper, Mowbray, Pallister and Gill to the likes of Parkinson, Hamilton, Kerr, Burke and Ripley and then to the goalscorers, Stephens and Slaven and Senior.

In those days, the Play-offs included the team that finished third from bottom of the League above, and that year it was Chelsea. Bernie scored again, adding to a Trevor Senior goal to win the first leg at Ayresome Park. The heroes held on at Stamford Bridge, losing 1–0 but completing an aggregate victory. Middlesbrough Football Club were promoted back to the First Division after a traumatic six-year absence, and Chelsea were relegated. Different days? They certainly were. But before we could enjoy any of it the dreaded summer of 1986 still had to be endured.

Opposite: Bernie Slaven, hero of the Holgate End.

Summer of 1986 and the Ayresome Park gates are locked. We thought it might be forever.

Summer Liquidation

(1986)

These are my memories of summer, 1986: An azure sea lapping golden sands as the sun beamed down from a cloudless sky. Yes, another family holiday in Whitby was about to be devastated by the news that Boro had gone into liquidation. The club had effectively ceased to exist, and there was also the realisation that Saturday afternoons would be changed forever, because you do not choose a club to support, the club chooses you. Without it you could

The key was in the hands of the official receiver, but help was on its way.

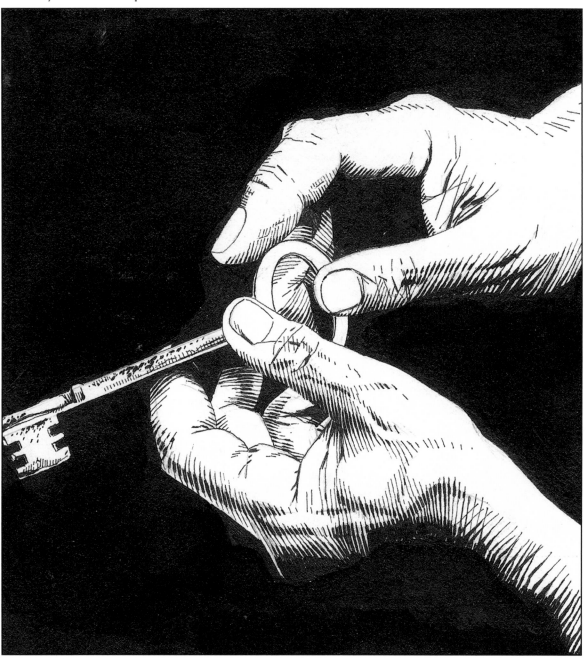

not simply switch your allegiance to a more prosperous outfit. A love for the game might maintain a disinterested viewing of *Match of the Day*, but the passion would be gone. Then it was whispered that Boro could survive and had applied to join the Conference. There was even a perverse pleasure, if it had to be that way, in the idea of working our way back up the divisions from non-League football.

Fortunately, the cavalry was coming. At least as the announcement was made that a new Middlesbrough FC would survive. I am fairly certain there was the distant sound of trumpets as they rose phoenix-like from the ashes of liquidation. Bruce Rioch was manager and Tony Mowbray his captain, uniting the players into an irresistible youthful force in those heady days of rejuvenation. The first major step was promotion back to Division Two, and it was achieved on 6 May 1987 in a goalless draw at Ayresome Park against Wigan Athletic.

Twenty years later, that fledgling club has come a long way from the irresistible force that Bruce Rioch initiated. One step forward, two steps back at times, as the years passed and new managerial teams followed.

Every one of them achieved something, and not many clubs can say that of six successive managers. Bruce set the ball rolling and Colin Todd followed; possibly overlooked historically, he at least took us to the Play-offs. Then Lennie Lawrence made sure we were part of the inaugural Premiership. With Bryan Robson it was the beginning of the Riverside rollercoaster, Terry Venables helping to ensure that the wheels did not fall off. And Steve McClaren then delivered silverware.

All this was a long way from 1986, when existence was enough to be grateful for, and there was still a summer holiday to be endured.

Bruce Rioch

Middlesbrough manager (1986–90)

The name of Bruce Rioch is deeply etched in the Middlesbrough pantheon. His achievements as manager are the stuff that dreams are made of. It was all a good 14 years away though when, as an Aston Villa player, he held off the challenge of Boro's Nobby Stiles and Bill Gates at Villa Park on 28 October 1972. The game ended 1–1, and as the teams traipsed off the pitch it is doubtful if Bruce heard the clarion call of destiny. His playing career had still to take in spells at the likes of Derby County and Everton and even Seattle Sounders in the US and a place in the NASL Team of All-Stars.

He took over as manager at Middlesbrough after a brief spell in charge of Torquay in 1986, and the rest, of course, is history. He did, however, return to Villa to plunder their ranks for the likes of Paul Kerr, Dean Glover, Mark Burke, Kevin Poole etc, to bolster our own young team. This paved the way

Bruce Rioch was manager and Tony
Mowbray his captain.

Colin Todd was Bruce Rioch's number
two and would replace him as
manager in 1990.

for a later regime to acquire the likes of the incomparable Ugo, the mighty George, and the present incumbent of the managerial chair, Gareth.

All this helps explain something I once read. An Aston Villa supporter was quoted as saying that Boro were the one team they always wanted to beat because every close season they came sniffing round their players: 'Like the annoying bloke in the pub who won't leave your girlfriend alone. Except in our case, she always goes off with him.'

Bruce Rioch as a Villa player giving as many lumps as he is getting back to Boro's Nobby Stiles and Bill Gates.

Chapter Twelve

The 1990s Onwards

Opposite: Andy Peake, signed from Charlton, Alan Kernaghan, Boro captain, and Robbie Mustoe's winner against Millwall on the Middlesbrough managerial debut of the mastermind behind it all, Lennie Lawrence.

It was just as well that in 1991 Ayresome Park did not have revolving doors, because had it done so Lennie Lawrence and Alan Kernaghan might have missed each other as they went in opposite directions. As manager of Charlton Athletic, Lawrence had signed the player on loan during the previous season and, using all his persuasive powers, was on the verge of persuading Kernaghan to make the move permanent. The young defender prepared to say his goodbyes at the Boro and was probably slightly taken aback when he met the new manager who had just replaced Colin Todd. None other than Lennie Lawrence himself, who then had the task of undoing all his good work on behalf of Charlton and convince Kernaghan that it was actually a much better idea to stay in the North East. Which was true, because he went on to enjoy his best period as a Boro player, taking over the captaincy in November that year (his home debut in the role was a 2–0 victory over Charlton). He was then joined by another familiar face when Lawrence went back to plunder his old club and signed midfielder Andy Peake. The push for promotion continued and was successfully attained in typically nail-biting fashion with a 2–1 away victory at Wolves on the last day of the season. On 2 May 1992 Boro were promoted to the inaugural Premier League.

Lennie Lawrence's reign had started back on 17 August 1991, when Robbie Mustoe scored the winner against Millwall. And, just to complete the circle, after 351 appearances, including a record number of Premiership starts, Robbie eventually made the journey south, joining Charlton Athletic when he left Boro in the summer of 2002.

Below: As Middlesbrough player-manager, Bryan Robson was haunted by the ghost of his curly perm at West Bromwich Albion.

Bryan Robson

(1994–97) 25 appearances and Boro manager.
In the late 1970s and the beginning of the 1980s, a young footballer with the compulsory curly perm and moustache of the era was getting the supporters of West Bromwich Albion to sit up and take notice. In 1994, battle-scarred perhaps, but with less tonsurial eccentricity, he became player-manager at Ayresome Park.

Bryan Robson, taking over where Lennie Lawrence left off, started the revolution that took Middlesbrough back to the Premiership, as the First Division was now being called, and consolidated the team at a level that we now take for granted. And it should be noted that such consolidation might have

been for an even longer period if the FA had not docked three points in the 1996–97 season for 'failing to fulfil a fixture.' Had Boro enough fit players to put out a team, could there seriously be any doubt that they would have done so? In the end they were relegated by virtue of those lost points, and had it not been the case then Coventry City would have said goodbye to the top flight a lot earlier than they actually did so. Still, Bryan Robson brought the Boro straight back the very next season, and that is where they have been ever since.

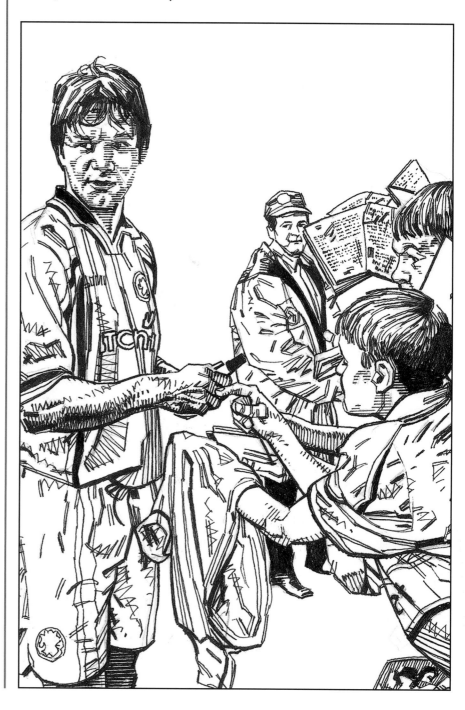

Uwe Fuchs, an early inspired Bryan Robson loan signing who, along with Fjortoft, Hignett, Hendrie et al, scored vital goals that assured promotion to the top flight in the last season at Ayresome Park.

'NO PLACE LIKE HOME...'

'STEPHEN PEARS' TESTIMONIAL WAS THE LAST GAME PLAYED AT AYRESOME PARK. BY 26 AUGUST 1995 THE RIVERSIDE STADIUM WAS OPEN FOR BUSINESS.'

'AS PEARS HAD SCORED THE LAST GOAL AT AYRESOME (A PENALTY, HE WAS A GOALKEEPER, AFTER ALL), CRAIG HIGNETT SCORED THE RIVERSIDE'S FIRST IN A 2-0 WIN OVER CHELSEA.'

'AND A WHOLE NEW ERA WAS UP AND RUNNING.'

'NEVER BETTER EXEMPLIFIED THAN BY GIANLUCA FESTA, IN TYPICALLY BULLISH MOOD, TAKING ON DEAN WINDASS (WHO JOINED BORO LATER THAT SEASON) OF BRADFORD CITY ON 25 NOVEMBER 2000.'

'THERE WERE NEW **HEROES**, OF COURSE.'

'FROM FAR, FAR AWAY.'

'SOME MORE SUCCESSFUL THAN OTHERS.'

'BUT THEY ALL PLAYED THEIR PART. SUCH AS NOEL WHELAN GIVING THE ARSENAL DEFENCE A TORRID TIME ON 4 NOVEMBER 2000 (WE LOST 1-0.)'

'AND CERTAIN STALWARTS REMAINED, SUCH AS CURTIS FLEMING, WHO WOULD HAVE HIS TESTIMONIAL GAME AT THE BEGINNING OF THE 2001-02 SEASON. A 3-0 VICTORY OVER ATHLETIC BILBAO.'

'NOT TO DENIGRATE THE BORO'S OLD TRAINING GROUND, HUTTON ROAD IN LONGLANDS, WHERE I SPENT MANY A HAPPY WINTER AFTERNOON WATCHING THE JUNIOR TEAM...'

'...BUT A STATE-OF-THE-ART FACILITY SUCH AS MIDDLESBROUGH FC'S ROCKCLIFFE PARK IS A PRETTY EMPHATIC STEP UP FROM A KICKABOUT IN THE PARK.'

'AND, AT THE BEGINNING OF THE 2000-01 SEASON, BRYAN ROBSON'S SEVENTH IN CHARGE, THERE WAS THE OPTIMISTIC FEELING THAT THINGS WERE LOOKING GOOD.'

'THERE WERE THREE OUTSTANDING GOALKEEPERS, MARLON BERESFORD REMAINED AS COVER FOR MARK SCHWARZER (ALONG WITH MARK CROSSLEY)...'

'...AND NEW FACES SUCH AS CAMEROON'S JOSEPH DESIRE JOB AND FRENCH INTERNATIONAL, CHRISTIAN KAREMBEU, WERE ON BOARD'

'LINING UP AND TAKING IT SERIOUSLY ALONGSIDE STEVE VICKERS, WHO HAD BEEN AT THE CLUB SINCE 1993 AND KEITH O'NEILL IN HIS SECOND SEASON.'

'THE YOUNG ARGENTINIAN, CARLOS MARINELLI, PREPARED TO DO BATTLE UNDER THE WATCHFUL EYE OF VETERAN STRIKER, BRIAN DEANE.'

'THE SUN WAS SHINING AND THE NEW SEASON APPROACHED. NOTHING COULD POSSIBLY GO WRONG.'

'UNFORTUNATELY, THINGS ARE RARELY THAT STRAIGHTFORWARD...'

'FATHERS AND SONS STILL CAME TO GAMES...'

'...EVEN IF THINGS WERE GOING BADLY. THERE WAS ALWAYS THE NEXT GAME AND THE OPPORTUNITY THAT MY GRANDAD WOULD HAVE UNDERSTOOD, 'TO GIVE THEM ONE MORE CHANCE!'

"ON 18 NOVEMBER 2000 UGO EHIOGU MADE HIS HOME DEBUT ON A BITTERLY COLD AFTERNOON AGAINST LEICESTER CITY.'

'DESPITE AWAY VICTORIES AT COVENTRY AND SOUTHAMPTON, BORO STILL HAD NOT WON AT HOME EXCEPT FOR THAT CLOSE-RUN CARLING CUP TIE AGAINST MACCLESFIELD.'

'THE CLOSEST WE GOT TO A GOAL WAS THE OCCASIONAL GOALMOUTH SCRAMBLE THAT INVARIABLY SAW THE BALL HOOFED TO SAFETY.'

'IT DID NOT GET ANY BETTER AGAINST LEICESTER.'

'WHILE VIV ANDERSON AND BRYAN ROBSON WERE TORMENTED ONLOOKERS AS EVERYTHING WENT HORRIBLY WRONG...'

'...AND LEICESTER SCORED THREE TIMES TO BORO'S NIL...'

'...FATHERS AND SONS WATCHED FROM THE STANDS AND TRIED TO REMEMBER BETTER DAYS.'

'WHILE IT WAS TRUE THAT THE CLUB HAD BEEN UNLUCKY AT TIMES AND LOST SOME GAMES BY THE ODD GOAL WHERE THEY MIGHT HAVE AT LEAST DESERVED A DRAW, THEY WERE IN TROUBLE NOW. THE QUESTION WAS, WHAT WERE THEY GOING TO DO ABOUT IT?'

'VIV ANDERSON HAD BEEN BRYAN ROBSON'S ASSISTANT AS THE CLUB HAD ESTABLISHED ITSELF IN THE TOP FLIGHT. THERE HAD BEEN THREE CUP FINALS IN THAT TIME. GREAT PLAYERS AND GREAT DRAMA. THE RIVERSIDE STADIUM HAD RISEN UP AND BEEN PACKED TO THE RAFTERS...'

'BRYAN ROBSON HIMSELF HAD TAKEN AN ORDINARY SECOND DIVISION SIDE AND TURNED IT INTO SOMETHING MANY OF US HAD BARELY DARED TO HOPE FOR: A PREMIERSHIP PHENOMENOM. HE WAS NOT ABOUT TO LET IT ALL JUST CRUMBLE AWAY.'

'AND HE WAS BRAVE ENOUGH TO ASK FOR HELP'

'IN EARLY DECEMBER, 2000, TERRY VENABLES AGREED TO JOIN THE FIGHT.'

'IF IT STARTED BADLY WITH YET ANOTHER UNLUCKY DEFEAT, 1-0 AWAY TO SUNDERLAND OF ALL PEOPLE, THE REAL TEST WOULD COME AT THE RIVERSIDE...'

'BORO WERE STILL WITHOUT A HOME WIN IN THE LEAGUE ON 16 DECEMBER WHEN CHELSEA CAME TO TOWN.'

'BUT THERE WAS STILL HOPE SO LONG AS THE BATTLING QUALITIES OF ROBBIE MUSTOE COULD INSPIRE OTHERS ON THE FIELD...'

'...LIKE GIANLUCA FESTA...'

'...OR PAUL OKON, THE AUSTRALIAN SWEEPER, AND YET ANOTHER REAL WARRIOR, COLIN COOPER.'

'THE GAME EBBED AND FLOWED...'

'...WITH NO ONE GETTING THE UPPER HAND AND THE MINUTES TICKING AWAY.'

'PERHAPS THERE WERE THOSE THAT THOUGHT A GOALLESS DRAW AGAINST THIS QUALITY OF OPPOSITION WAS NO BAD THING...'

'...BUT ROBSON AND VENABLES WERE NOT AMONG THEM.'

'WITH JUST OVER 20 MINUTES TO GO, THEY SENT ON SUBSTITUTE DEAN GORDON...'

'...WHO HIT A SHOT FROM WELL OUTSIDE THE BOX THAT TOOK A DEFLECTION AND NESTLED SNUGLY IN THE CHELSEA NET.'

'16 DECEMBER 2000, MIDDLESBROUGH 1 CHELSEA 0. HAPPY CHRISTMAS EVERYONE! VICTORIES OVER LIVERPOOL AND DERBY FOLLOWED, AND HARD-FOUGHT FOR POINTS WERE GAINED AWAY FROM HOME, INCLUDING A 3-0 VICTORY AT ARSENAL. AND THERE WAS EVEN GREATER CAUSE FOR REJOICING, BECAUSE ALEN BOKSIC WAS ABOUT TO COME GOOD...'

'...WITH VITAL GOALS IN VITAL GAMES, AND NONE MORE SATISFYING THAN THE PAIR HE GOT IN A 2-1 WIN AT NEWCASTLE IN MARCH. (MARK SCHWARZER ALSO SAVED A PENALTY. BORO DO HAVE A WAY OF KEEPING YOU ON THE EDGE OF YOUR SEAT.)'

'HE ENDED UP AS THE OFFICIAL PLAYER OF THE SEASON, AND THE TEAM SETTLED FOR A SAFE 14TH PLACE IN THE PREMIERSHIP TABLE.'

'NO-ONE IS SAYING ALEN DID NOT DESERVE HIS AWARD, PRESENTED TO HIM BY CHAIRMAN STEVE GIBSON AT THE START OF THE NEXT SEASON, BUT CREDIT IS EQUALLY DUE TO OTHERS. TO COOPER, MUSTOE, FLEMING AND INCE. TO PLAYERS LIKE THEM WHO GAVE THEIR HEARTS FOR THE BLOOD-RED SHIRT.'

'AND WE OWE AN EVEN BIGGER DEBT TO STEVE GIBSON, WHOSE COMMITMENT TO THE PROGRESS OF THE CLUB IS FUELLED BY HIS LOVE FOR IT.'

"SOMETIME LATER, GARETH SOUTHGATE WOULD HAVE THE LAST WORDS ON THE ENIGMA OF ALEN BOKSIC: "HE WENT WITHOUT SAYING GOODBYE...WHAT DID MIDDLESBROUGH MEAN TO HIM? FROM HIS YACHT ON THE DALMATIAN COAST, WILL HE FOLLOW BORO'S RESULTS?""

'ROBSON AND VENABLES DEPARTED AT THE END OF THE PREVIOUS SEASON. AN ERA HAD ENDED AND A NEW ONE WAS ABOUT TO BEGIN.'

'STEVE MCCLAREN, MIDDLESBROUGH MANAGER, 2001–2004.'

'AND WHAT AN ERA IT WAS GOING TO BE!'

'GARETH SOUTHGATE, A LEADER IN WAITING IF EVER THERE WAS ONE, MADE HIS MIDDLESBROUGH DEBUT IN THE 2001-02 SEASON. AS DID A YOUNG FRENCHMAN WHO, ON ONLY HIS SECOND APPEARANCE AND FIRST AT THE RIVERSIDE, SCORED AGAINST SUNDERLAND.'

'AFTER ONLY TWO MINUTES HE OUT-JUMPED THE SUNDERLAND DEFENCE TO WIN A HEADER...'

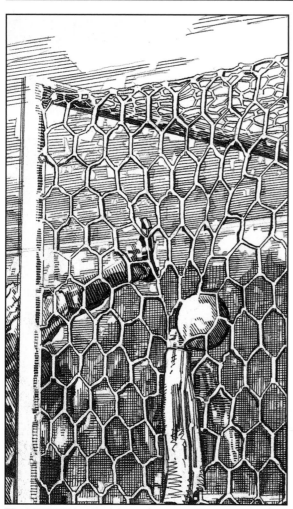

'...THE BALL LOOPING HIGH INTO THE NIGHT SKY BEFORE BOUNCING DOWN INTO THE GOAL.'

'WELCOME TO THE RIVERSIDE, FRANCK QUEDURUE!'

'ON 3 NOVEMBER WE ALSO WELCOMED BACK AN OLD FAVOURITE...'

'...BUT NOW FABRIZIO RAVANELLI WAS IN THE COLOURS OF DERBY COUNTY.'

'BUT THE DAY WAS A RARE GOOD ONE FOR THE BOY FROM ARGENTINA.'

'CARLOS MARINELLI CELEBRATED THE FIRST OF HIS GOALS IN A RESTRAINED FASHION...'

'...THOUGH HE LET HIS EMOTIONS GET THE BETTER OF HIM WHEN NUMBER TWO WENT IN. BORO WON 5-1. (FABRIZIO, INEVITABLY, GOT THE CONSOLATION FOR DERBY.)'

'THEN THERE WERE THE BATTLES WITH THE MASTER.'

'STEVE MCCLAREN HAD BEEN ALEX FERGUSON'S NUMBER TWO AT MANCHESTER UNITED UP TO AND DURING THEIR INCREDIBLE TREBLE-WINNING SEASON IN 1999, SO IT WAS INEVITABLE THAT IT WOULD GIVE EXTRA SPICE TO THEIR ENCOUNTERS AS RIVAL BOSSES.'

'ON 15 DECEMBER 2001 UNITED WERE AT THE RIVERSIDE AND IN NO MOOD TO LET A RESURGENT MIDDLESBROUGH HAVE THINGS THEIR OWN WAY.'

'SOLSKJAER WAS A THORN IN THE SIDE...OR A PAIN IN THE ARSE...DEPENDING WHERE YOUR LOYALTIES LAY...(GREAT PLAYER THOUGH.)'

'AND AS ROY KEANE MADE A VERY GOOD ATTEMPT TO SEPARATE BORO KEEPER MARK CROSSLEY'S HEAD FROM HIS SHOULDERS...'

'...IT IS DOUBTFUL IF HE EVER SPARED A THOUGHT FOR THE FACT THAT THEY HAD BOTH ONCE BEEN NOTTINGHAM FOREST PLAYERS.'

'IN FACT THERE WERE OLD TEAMMATES EVERYWHERE YOU LOOKED THAT DAY.'

'FROM OUT ON THE PITCH WITH PAUL INCE, ONCE THE GUV'NOR OF MANCHESTER UNITED...'

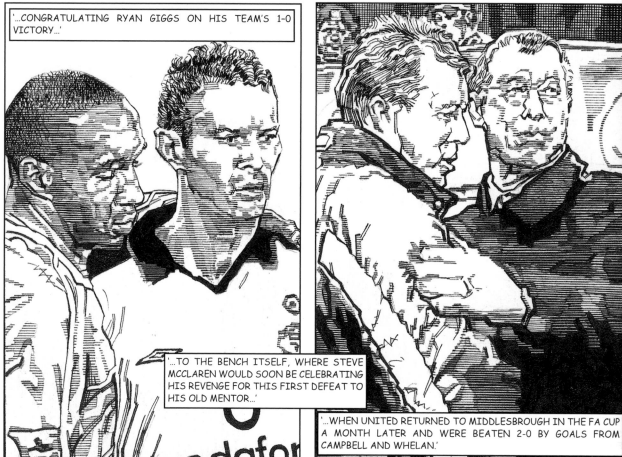

'...CONGRATULATING RYAN GIGGS ON HIS TEAM'S 1-0 VICTORY...'

'...TO THE BENCH ITSELF, WHERE STEVE MCCLAREN WOULD SOON BE CELEBRATING HIS REVENGE FOR THIS FIRST DEFEAT TO HIS OLD MENTOR...'

'...WHEN UNITED RETURNED TO MIDDLESBROUGH IN THE FA CUP A MONTH LATER AND WERE BEATEN 2-0 BY GOALS FROM CAMPBELL AND WHELAN.'

'BORO WOULD ALSO GO TO OLD TRAFFORD LATER THAT SEASON AND WIN 1–0 WITH YET ANOTHER VITAL ALEN BOKSIC GOAL. WHICH PUT STEVE 2–1 UP IN THE HEAD-TO-HEADS.'

'STEVE MCCLAREN'S FIRST SEASON IN CHARGE CERTAINLY HAD ITS MOMENTS. AND ANOTHER ONE WAS CELEBRATED BY GARETH SOUTHGATE AND FRANCK QUEDURUE AS THE FRENCHMAN GRABS AN EQUALISER FROM A FREE-KICK AGAINST SPURS ON 30 MARCH 2002.
THERE WAS AN EXHILARATING CUP RUN, TOO, THAT TOOK US ALL THE WAY TO THE SEMI-FINALS AND A LESS HAPPY RETURN TO OLD TRAFFORD, WHERE ARSENAL WERE WAITING. A 1–0 DEFEAT WAS NO DISGRACE THOUGH, WITH HALF THE BORO TEAM INJURED AND WITH GOOD LUCK A STRANGER TO US. IT WAS AN EARLY INDICATION HOWEVER, THAT GOOD CUP RUNS WERE SOMETHING OF A SPECIALITY FOR STEVE MCCLAREN.'

'THE NEXT SEASON FEATURED MASSIMO MACCARONE SCORING TWICE ON HIS HOME LEAGUE DEBUT AGAINST FULHAM AT THE RIVERSIDE ON 24 AUGUST.'

'WE WERE 2-0 UP AND IN CONTROL UNTIL THE LAST MINUTES OF INJURY TIME WHEN THE CRAVEN COTTAGE TEAM SCORED TWICE.'

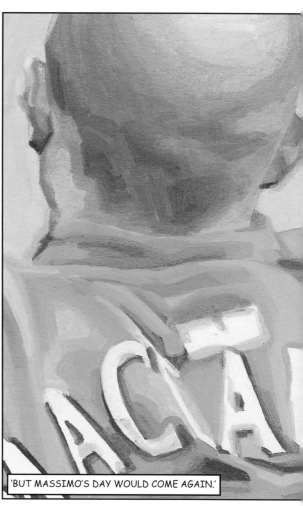

'BUT MASSIMO'S DAY WOULD COME AGAIN.'

'A HAPPIER AFTERNOON WAS SPENT AGAINST BLACKBURN ROVERS JUST SEVEN DAYS LATER, WHEN IT WAS THE BORO'S TURN TO CELEBRATE LAST-MINUTE DRAMA.'

'JOSEPH DESIRE JOB SLIDING IN TO SCORE THE ONLY GOAL OF THE GAME WITH JUST SECONDS OF PLAY REMAINING.'

'HE CELEBRATED WELL ENOUGH THAT DAY...'

'...UNAWARE THAT LADY DESTINY HAD SOMETHING EVEN BETTER UP HER SLEEVE, JUST A YEAR OR SO IN THE FUTURE.'

'MEANWHILE, GARETH SOUTHGATE HAD TAKEN OVER THE CAPTAINCY FROM PAUL INCE...'

'...AND LED BY EXAMPLE, EVEN IF IT MEANT MATCHING THE BANDAGED WRATH OF HARRY KEWELL OF LEEDS UNITED ON 26 OCTOBER 2003.'

'WITH FRANCK QUEDURUE STANDING BY TO OFFER SUPPORT, GARETH PUT HIS POINT ACROSS.'

'THEN UNDERLINED IT BY SCORING AN EQUALISING GOAL IN A 2-2 DRAW.'

'IN FACT, GARETH SOUTHGATE WAS NOT ADVERSE TO NOTCHING THE OCCASIONAL GOAL, AS AGAINST LIVERPOOL IN THE NEXT HOME GAME.'

'JERZY DUDEK, THE LIVERPOOL KEEPER RUSHES OUT TO GRAB THE BALL...'

'...SEEMS TO HAVE IT UNDER CONTROL AS HE FALLS TO EARTH...'

'...BUT IT SLIPS FROM HIS GRASP AND PRESENTS GARETH WITH THE OPPORTUNITY TO SCORE...'

'MIDDLESBROUGH 1 LIVERPOOL 0.'

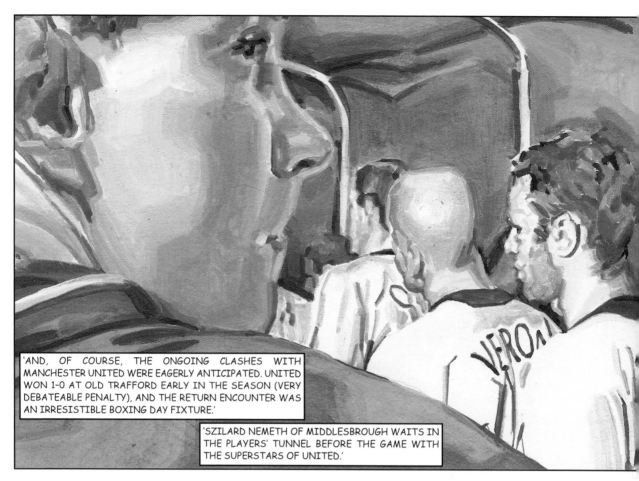

'AND, OF COURSE, THE ONGOING CLASHES WITH MANCHESTER UNITED WERE EAGERLY ANTICIPATED. UNITED WON 1-0 AT OLD TRAFFORD EARLY IN THE SEASON (VERY DEBATEABLE PENALTY), AND THE RETURN ENCOUNTER WAS AN IRRESISTIBLE BOXING DAY FIXTURE.'

'SZILARD NEMETH OF MIDDLESBROUGH WAITS IN THE PLAYERS' TUNNEL BEFORE THE GAME WITH THE SUPERSTARS OF UNITED.'

'AS GIGGS AND NEMETH TAKE TO THE FIELD A MEMORABLE YULETIDE LIES AHEAD. BOKSIC WILL SCORE FOR BORO, THEN NEMETH A SECOND, BEFORE GIGGS PULLS ONE BACK FOR UNITED.'

'THEN MORE HEROICS FROM JOB AND BORO WIN THE GAME 3-1. ANOTHER HAPPY CHRISTMAS. OR, AS TINY TIM MIGHT HAVE PUT IT: "GOD BLESS 'EM. EVERY ONE!'

'AND SO THE DAYS PASS UNTIL WE GET TO 24 AUGUST 2003 AND, AS GARETH PREPARES TO LEAD THE TEAM OUT FOR AN OPENING FIXTURE AGAINST ARSENAL, BEHIND HIM JENS LEHMANN AND MARK SCHWARZER SWAP TALES ABOUT LIFE IN THE GERMAN BUNDESLIGA...'

'...A REMARKABLE SEASON IS ABOUT TO BEGIN.'

'NOT THAT YOU WOULD HAVE APPRECIATED THE FACT BY TEA TIME THAT DAY, AFTER WHICH, DESPITE THE PLEASANTRIES SHARED BY THE TWO BRAZILIANS, DORIVA OF MIDDLESBROUGH AND GILBERTO OF ARSENAL, IT WAS THE LATTER WHO WOULD HAVE MOST TO SMILE ABOUT AFTER A 4-0 VICTORY.'

ONE OF THE KEY INGREDIENTS OF THE SUCCESS WE ENJOYED IN THE 2003-04 SEASON WAS THE RETURN TO FORM OF JUNINHO, NOW IN HIS THIRD SPELL AT MIDDLESBROUGH.

Juninho

It is amazing how time flies. In October 1995 Boro signed Brazilian Player of the Year Juninho for the first time from São Paulo. Was it really that long ago? Of course, the magic he wove round the Riverside has long since passed into folklore. It is unforgettable for all the highs and lows which accompanied that rollercoaster time, and every bit as irresistible.

Middlesbrough v Bolton Wanderers

Carling Cup Final (29 February 2004).

The road there and the game itself…sometimes words are not enough.

'HIGHBURY, 20 JANUARY 2004, CARLING CUP SEMI-FINAL – FIRST LEG. ARSENAL HAVE BEEN HABITUALLY BEATING MIDDLESBROUGH THROUGHOUT THE MCCLAREN YEARS IN WHATEVER COMPETITION OUR PATHS HAVE CROSSED, MOST MEMORABLY IN THE FA CUP SEMI-FINAL OF 2002…'

'BUT YOU JUST FELT, AS SOON AS JUNINHO'S SHOT WENT INTO THE NET, THAT THIS TIME, JUST FOR ONCE, THINGS WERE GOING TO BE DIFFERENT.'

'AND SO IT PROVED. WE WON THE SECOND LEG 2-1, AND MIDDLESBROUGH FOOTBALL CLUB HAD REACHED THE CARLING CUP FINAL.'

'EVER SINCE 23 APRIL 1898, WHEN BORO HAD LAST WON THE FA AMATEUR CUP, THEIR APPEARANCES IN MAJOR CUP FINALS HAD BEEN A DISAPPOINTMENT. FOUR APPEARANCES IN EITHER THE ZENITH DATA SYSTEMS, LEAGUE OR FA CUP HAD MEANT AS MANY DEFEATS, TO CHELSEA (THREE TIMES) AND LEICESTER CITY (AFTER A REPLAY), BUT NOT THIS TIME.'

'AS GARETH SOUTHGATE AND JUNINHO AND THE REST OF TEESSIDE ERUPTED WITH DELIGHT, IT WAS HARD NOT TO BRUSH AWAY A MANLY TEAR.'

'CARLING CUP FINAL, MILLENIUM STADIUM, CARDIFF, 29 FEBRUARY 2004, MIDDLESBROUGH 2 BOLTON WANDERERS 1.'

'JOSEPH DESIRE JOB HAD MET LADY DESTINY AND PUT BORO ONE UP. BOLO ZENDEN CONVERTED A PENALTY TO MAKE IT 2-0, THEN WANDERERS PULLED ONE BACK. IT WAS A PULSATING GAME. BORO WITH THE UPPER HAND AS IT WENT ON AND ASSUMING THE GREATER PART OF CONTROL, BUT NEVERTHELESS MARK SCHWARZER HAD TO MAKE AT LEAST THREE OUT-OF-THIS-WORLD SAVES.'

'SO WHY SHOULD TWO MEN OF THE MATCH NOT SEEK EACH OTHER OUT AFTER THE FINAL WHISTLE? IN FACT, THERE WERE 11 MEN OF THE MATCH AND THEIR NAMES WERE: 'SCHWARZER, MILLS, EHIOGU, QUEDURUE, DORIVA, BOATENG, ZENDEN, MENDIETA, JUNINHO, JOB...AND THE SUBSTITUTES, RICKETTS (WHO HAD EQUALISED AWAY TO SPURS), DOWNING, MACCARONE, RIGGOTT AND JONES...'

'...ALL LED ON THE FIELD BY A GREAT CAPTAIN...A GREAT LEADER...'

'...AND OFF IT, BY THE FIRST MANAGER (SO FAR) OF MODERN TIMES TO DELIVER SILVERWARE TO MIDDLESBROUGH FOOTBALL CLUB.'

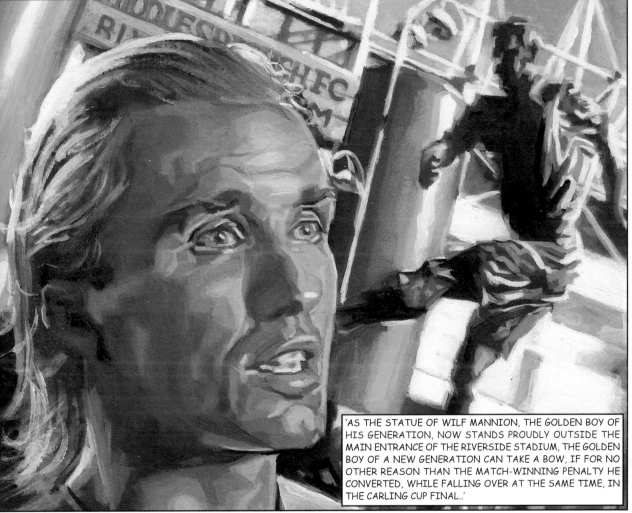

'AS THE STATUE OF WILF MANNION, THE GOLDEN BOY OF HIS GENERATION, NOW STANDS PROUDLY OUTSIDE THE MAIN ENTRANCE OF THE RIVERSIDE STADIUM, THE GOLDEN BOY OF A NEW GENERATION CAN TAKE A BOW, IF FOR NO OTHER REASON THAN THE MATCH-WINNING PENALTY HE CONVERTED, WHILE FALLING OVER AT THE SAME TIME, IN THE CARLING CUP FINAL..'

'IF NOT EXACTLY LAUDED IN THE SAME WAY AS THE IMMORTAL WILF (THE TERRACE CHANT WENT SOMETHING LIKE, 'HE USED TO BE SHITE, BUT NOW HE'S ALRIGHT, BOLO, BOLO ZENDEN...'), AND EVEN THOUGH HE DID NOT STAY VERY LONG AFTER THE NEXT SEASON'S EUROPEAN ADVENTURE, AT LEAST HE AND JOSEPH DESIRE JOB GOT THE GOALS THAT TOOK US THERE.'

Colin Cooper

I can always remember where I was and what I was doing at the time by the movies I watched along the way. So, when I think of Colin Cooper, I remember the fresh-faced youngster who made his debut in the 1985–86 season. At the time there was film in the cinema called *The Goonies*, which revelled in the exuberance of youth as it triumphed over adversity. It was the story of a group of disparate youngsters who set out on the adventure of a lifetime. There was a youthful zest up there on the screen that was reflected in Boro's irresistible march from the heartbreak of liquidation in 1986 through divisions two and three, all the way to the First Division in successive

Colin Cooper after his return to Middlesbrough. Now part of manager Gareth Southgate's management team.

Jimmy Floyd
Hasselbaink.

seasons. During which time, Colin Cooper was growing up and was more or less ever present in the side until the end of 1989, when injury kept him out of the last three games of a season that saw the dream start to die.

In a team that was losing its youthful fire, his games became less regular until the end of 1991 when a measly £300,000 took him to Millwall. In 1991 cinema audiences were enthralled by *Robin Hood: Prince of Thieves*, and some of the swashbuckling fire rubbed off on Colin Cooper, despite a 1–0 defeat against Boro (football has a way of doing things like that), on his Millwall debut. After only a few games, his star was back in the ascendancy, and Millwall made a massive profit of £1,400,000 when they sold him just a couple of years later. Somewhat appropriately, his new club was a near neighbour of Sherwood, the greenwood home of Robin Hood: Nottingham Forest.

In *Jurassic Park*, arguably, the movie of 1993, audiences watched the revival of dinosaurs long since extinct. At the same time Forest, with Cooper in their ranks, were on the verge of resurrecting some of their former glory. Relegated from the Premier League in the previous season, they won instant promotion back to the top flight, followed by European qualification. Colin Cooper, with the tenacity of a reborn velociraptor, was becoming battle hardened, and a couple of England appearances were the least he deserved.

In 1998, the movie *Patch Adams* had among its opening lines: 'All of life is a coming home…All the restless hearts of the world, all trying to find a way home.' It was the year a warrior returned to the place where it all began. Colin Cooper was back at the Boro.

And who will ever forget: Jimmy Floyd Hasselbaink? He is pictured at Blackburn on 16 October 2004, where he scored a hat-trick in a 4–0 win. Or Mark Viduka? Yet another great goalscorer celebrating one of his two goals that ending a barren period on 6 December 2004 as Middlesbrough beat Manchester City 3–2. Goal drought? What goal drought?

Mark Viduka.

Gareth Southgate

Familiar celebratory stance but an unfamiliar team shirt? Well, there is quite a good explanation:

Steve Coppell, manager of Reading Football Club, was one of the great players of his day, and watching awestruck as he wove his magic on the wing for Manchester United and England was a young supporter of the Reds whose name was Gareth Southgate. So, it was quite appropriate that a few years later Steve Coppell, by then in charge of Crystal Palace, should give Gareth his first-team debut (after 120 reserve-team games) in the 1990–91 season. It led to the Palace team clinching promotion on 1 May 1994 and Gareth scoring the opening goal in a 3–2 victory at Ayresome Park of all places (the swine!). He then commenced, along with Chris Coleman (now manager of Coventry City FC), to practice the well-known salutation that, a few years later, we would all come to love. Unfortunately, there were a couple of relegations either side of that triumph for Palace, but at least Gareth was on his way to Aston Villa and England and consistent performances at the very highest level. If one of the highlights of the early part of his career was that May day on Teesside in the 1990s, then the road

Inevitably the sun sets on the careers of all great players, and they must look forward to the challenges ahead.

Familiar celebratory
stance but an
unfamiliar team shirt?
Well, there's quite a
good explanation…

would eventually lead Gareth back to Middlesbrough. He could clean the mud off his boots for the last time, confident in the knowledge that the Boro team he came to play for, to captain and then to manage had achieved much more than we would ever have dreamed possible in those distant days. Personally, one cannot shake the feeling that his managerial legacy might well turn out to be every bit as memorable.

Steve Coppell.

Challenges do not come much bigger than this: Gareth Southgate as Middlesbrough manager.

Chapter Thirteen
Middlesbrough in Europe

Steve Bloomer, in agreement with Boro strikers Ravanelli and Boksic of a later century, thought that if certain players were on the ball, it was not worth making a run because they would not be able to deliver it.

Never listen to those deluded souls who will tell you that Middlesbrough have no European pedigree. As long ago as 1908 the club was on its second Danish tour in as many years. In June they faced a Denmark XI who included in their ranks Sophus Nielsen. Just a few months later, in October, he was the scorer of 10 goals in one game – a 17–1 demolition of France in the Olympic football tournament in London. Also among the Danes was Harold Bohr, reputedly the cleverer brother of Niels, who dreamed up the Quantum Theory of Atomic Structure. So there were one or two brains out there on the pitch too.

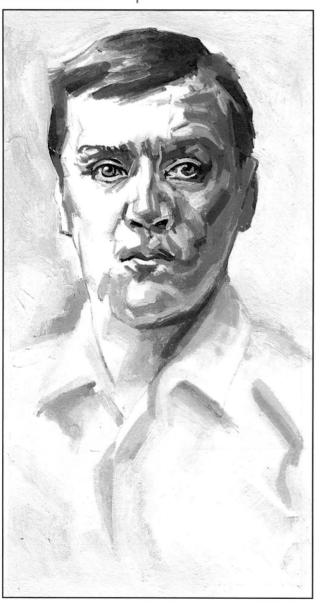

All of which makes it even more laudable that Boro won the game 5–2, with two goals from the great England international Steve Bloomer, two more from John Hall and a fifth from Sammy Cail. Steve 'Paleface' Bloomer, in common with Fabrizio Ravanelli, played for both Middlesbrough and Derby County and had a similar cold stare of disapproval for offending teammates who failed to deliver the right sort of pass. His own motto was, 'I try to get there first', and the least he expected was for the ball to be waiting for him. He was also a successful baseball player, winning the English Baseball Cup three times in the 1890s. That was when he was not too busy being a more-than-adequate amateur cricketer. And, while sponsorship is taken for granted nowadays, Bloomer led the way with his endorsements for Bloomers Lucky Strikers' Football Boots and Phosferine Tonic (Phosferine Tonic? Your guess is as good as mine). He is pictured in the white shirt winning a header in the Danish goalmouth, while the Middlesbrough player looking on is Fred Pentland. Both men later further cemented Boro's emerging continental connections when they subsequently took up coaching positions in Europe. Unfortunately, the country they chose to pursue this in was Germany, which might have been a bit unwise considering World War One was on the horizon.

Bloomer, in the white shirt, wins a header in the Danish goalmouth. The Boro player looking on is Fred Pentland.

Pentland and Bloomer celebrate the arrival in camp of a new football.

Fred Pentland, 'El Bombin,' in his lucky bowler hat.

At least the pair of them were interred together for the duration, along with 4,000 others, in the Ruhleben Camp near Berlin, and could swap tales about how they ran rings around the rest of the First Division in the 1908–09 season. The picture shows Pentland and Bloomer celebrating the arrival in camp of a new football.

While remaining in captivity, along with a handful of other professional players, they set up their own Football Association, playing League matches on a nearby racecourse. There was even a camp newspaper to report on it all. And, slightly more fortuitously, as those dark days wore on, at least no one was shooting at them.

Other Middlesbrough players, such as rising star Andy Jackson, Archie Wilson and Don McLeod, were not so fortunate. The war claimed their lives as it claimed so many others, leaving a scar across Europe that would never truly heal. Others of course, were marked forever. Did Walter Tinsley ever really recover fully from the gas attack he had to endure in the trenches? Then there was Andy Wilson, who would become Middlesbrough's top scorer in the 1921–22 and 1923–24, who always played with a black glove covering the hand that was maimed when a German shell exploded near him in 1918 (he did not let the injury prevent him playing bowls for England either). Even so, it was a far from idyllic existence that Steve Bloomer and Fred Pentland enjoyed in Ruhleben Camp, and Bloomer himself later referred to the place as 'that shit-hole.'

The two men found their way to France after hostilities ceased and, while Bloomer successfully coached Real Irun, Pentland really came into his own in charge of Racing Santander then Athletic Bilbao, earning himself the nickname 'El Bombin' (the Bowler Hat) – so-called because he always wore the bowler hat that his match-winning teams used to stamp on for luck. It must have worked because he won five Spanish titles in seven seasons, had brief spells at Atletico Madrid and Real Oviedo and also managed the first national Spanish team to beat England 4–3 in Madrid on 15 May 1929. Middlesborough player George Camsell missed the game through injury, but it still goes to show that, nearly 100 years ago, Boro's European credentials were well and truly established.

George Hardwick
(1937–50) 166 appearances.
In 1956 George Hardwick, who had represented Middlesbrough, England and Great Britain, even further extended his hometown club's links with Europe. He was director of coaching and national-team manager of the Netherlands and introduced the Total Football system to their emerging young players. It was a sporting philosophy embraced by those who followed him and had its rewards in 1974 and 1978 when the Holland team reached consecutive World Cup Finals. And the PSV Eindhoven team that came to Ayresome Park to play a floodlit friendly in March 1958 was managed by none other than George himself. Even so, his heart always remained on Teesside.

George Hardwick, captain of Middlesbrough, England and Great Britain.

'I do wish my old club well in the immediate future,' he said. 'And trust that they will eventually find the right blend of players to wear the famous blood-red shirt with pride and reward the faithful Boro supporters with their first major trophy. It's long, long, long overdue. I only hope it happens in my lifetime.'

On 29 February 2004, Middlesbrough Football Club won the Carling Cup, beating Bolton Wanderers 2–1 at The Cardiff Millennium Stadium, winning their first major trophy since the 19th Century, and, at the same time, qualifying for European competition in the UEFA Cup the following season. George Hardwick died just under two months later on 19 April 2004.

Boro v AS Roma

UEFA Cup Round 16 (9 February 2006). In 753 BC, so legend has it, Romulus and Remus decided that they had had enough of mother howling at the moon (she was a wolf after all), and it was time they should set out and build the city of Rome. At that same moment, give or take a decade or two, the Iron Age was what everyone in Britain was talking about. Cleveland itself was largely populated by the Brigante tribe, in isolated farming communities served by two roads.

The one road, Old Gat, carried market ware from the settlement of Iarhusum on the banks of the Tees to those tribal communities that lived in the Cleveland hills. Hol Gat intersected this road, travelling from north to south from the Tees, close to the hollow where Ayresome Park would be built, following the

Above: Associazione Sportiva Roma, fresh faced and eager for the 1927–28 season.

Opposite: Romulus and Remus. (And mother.)

Left: Billy Pease and George Camsell also ready for whatever 1927 had in store.

modern course of Ayresome Green Lane and then Roman Road. It became part of a road later adapted by the Romans and subsumed by them in their own convoys from the river, though it predated their occupation.

Apart from that, nothing much else was happening in Old Cleveland except for the occasional smelly druid passing through. There was not really a lot to shout about in football terms in either Middlesbrough or Rome and was not going to be for a few hundred years. But, by July 1927 (AD) things had really got going. Romulus and Remus now adorned the club badge on the Imperial red coloured shirts of the newly founded Associazione Sportiva Roma. AS Roma played at the Motovelodromo Appio in those days and are pictured fresh-faced and eager for the 1927–28 season. 1927 was also a historic year for Middlesbrough Football Club. They won promotion as Second Division champions and had legends of their own who were starting to hit the headlines. Winger Billy Pease made his debut at the beginning of the 1926–27 season, and the emerging gifts of George Camsell were setting Ayresome Park alight. The pair would go on to make over 600 League appearances between them in the Boro's blood-red shirt.

FC Basel lining up in 1900.

Percy Humphries in his
Tottenham days.

Middlesbrough v FC Basel

UEFA Cup Quarter-Final (6 April 2006).

When Fussball Club Basel was founded in November 1893, they were far from the professional outfit that would win the Swiss Cup for the first time in 1933 and the Championship in 1953. In fact, for the first 20 years of their existence they never got round to what might have seemed the simple formality of appointing an official coach. As they lined up for the 1900 season, the man who would eventually take on that role was making his career debut over 400 miles away for Queen's Park Rangers in the Southern League.

Percy Humphries losing out in a clash with Alf Common at Ayresome Park, 26 February 1909.

Just to digress for a second: If you look over the shoulder of Doctor Pfeiffer on the far left of the team line up (on page 182) you will see a hoarding (does it really say 'Cleveland'?) that seems to hint at an early connection with the North East of England. And that is really not as far-fetched an idea as you might think, which is where Percy Humphries comes in.

By the time that the 1913–14 season came around, the man in question had made his name at Notts County, Leicester Fosse, Chelsea and Spurs and moved on to become player-manager in the North Eastern League for Hartlepools, where injuries were starting to restrict his career. In May 1913 he took his coaching skills abroad, specifically to none other than FC Basel, where he remained until the end of that season.

Percy had played at Ayresome Park, of course. On 26 February 1909 he was a member of the Spurs team that lost 4–3 to Middlesbrough, and he is pictured losing out in a clash with Alf Common.

Middlesbrough v FC Steaua Bucharest
UEFA Cup Semi-Final (27 April 2006).
In January 1947 Middlesbrough FC was embarking on an FA Cup run that would end in quarter-final calamity at Burnley. But optimism was still unbridled

when Queen's Park Rangers fell victim to a 3–1 defeat in the third-round replay at Ayresome Park. Micky Fenton scored with a thumping header, then added a second before Wilf Mannion finished the scoring. Later that same year, the first Romanian Football League was underway, and among the participants were the newly formed Army Sports Association. Perhaps the club was not quite so romantically christened as it might have been and, with this in mind, the next year they changed their name to Army Central Sports Club, which really was not a lot better. Nevertheless, they went on to win the Romanian Cup in 1949. Then they changed their name again.

This time they became Army Central House, but it still was not getting any easier to come up with a good terrace chant. They won the Championship in 1951 and the Cup again, repeated the feat in 1952 and retained the League title in 1953. In 1961 they were champions again and, since it was a good 10 years since their last name change, finally settled on calling themselves Steaua (Star) Bucharest.

There are a couple of not-so-tenuous connections between them and Middlesbrough Football Club that showed up in the following years. In 1986, nearly 15 years before he and Bryan Robson steered Boro to Premiership survival, Terry Venables was the coach of Barcelona as they lost the Champions League Final,

Terry Venables of Barcelona and Boro.

missing all their penalties in a shoot-out with Steaua Bucharest, who became the first Eastern European club to win the trophy. And the former Steaua player Dan Petrescu was a member of the Chelsea team that compounded yet more Boro FA Cup heartbreak when they won the Final against the blood-reds in 1997.

So confidence was high in the Bucharest camp when they came to the Riverside Stadium in April 2006. They had a one-goal advantage from the first leg in Romania, which they had celebrated as if it was a job done, and almost before the second leg had settled itself they scored two more vital away goals. Boro were 3–0 down on aggregate, just as they had been in the quarter-final against Basel. Lightning could not strike twice. Or could it? First of all Massimo Maccarone pulled one back. Just a consolation. Or was it? In the second half Mark Viduka scored, and the stadium started to rock. The previous weekend, Chris Riggott had missed what looked like a sitter that would have levelled an FA Cup semi-final against West Ham that the Hammers won 1–0. This time he made no mistake, and the UEFA semi-final was level. But Steaua Bucharest still would go through to the Final on the away-goals-count-double rule unless something spectacular happened.

Micky Fenton scores against QPR.

Count Dracula.

I remember thinking what a terrible joke it was even as Stewart Downing wove down the left wing, controlling a rebound and preparing himself on the edge of the Steaua penalty area in the last minute of the game. Bucharest is historically in part of the Wallachia, Transylvania and Moldovia regions that were ruled in the 15th century by Vlad Tepes, whom Bram Stoker (writing it on holiday in Whitby, just up the road from Middlesbrough) based his Dracula character on. So, it was worth bearing in mind as Stewart's boot flashed around the ball that their team might not be very good at dealing with crosses. And Massimo Maccarone delivered a far more emphatic punchline.

They will tell you that Boro were outclassed by Seville in the Final that the Spaniards won 4–0. It is not true. The truth is that Middlesbrough Football Club were one goal down at half-time at the end of a season in which they had played 64 games, more than any other Premiership team in history. They were carrying injuries, and could there really have been yet another superhuman effort to save the game just as in the quarter-final and the semi-final? Yes, of course there could have been. If the Seville goalkeeper had not saved brilliantly from Viduka early in the second half or if the referee had given the penalty we should have had a few minutes later…who knows? Would hearts have found the strength for one last surge?

20 January 2007. Woodgate, Xavier and Downing celebrate a 5–1 win over Bolton Wanderers. But all things pass and only ghosts are left behind…

As it was, exhaustion took its toll. Seville finished it off in the last quarter of a game they had not dominated, no matter what anybody says. It goes back to the words of Danny Blanchflower, the captain of Tottenham Hotspur in the 1960s and a man who understood the drama of the game.

'The great fallacy is that the game is first and last about winning. It is nothing of the sort. Football is about glory, it is about doing things in style and with a flourish, about going out and beating the other lot, not waiting for them to die of boredom.'

And Massimo Maccarone's last-minute diving header against Steaua Bucharest was glorious.

Chapter Fourteen
Ghosts

On 11 May 2008, in the aftermath of a sizzling 8–1 victory over Manchester City, the Middlesbrough supporters have made their way home from the Riverside Stadium. The players have departed and the season has closed. The ground lies still under the lights until they too flicker and go out. Only moonbeams remain to illuminate the early summer night.

Two shades drift down from the steep south-east corner of the stands. Almost hesitantly at first, they move out onto the playing area. Someone has left a ball out on the pitch, and they are drawn to it irresistibly. If their shapes were uncertain before, they now become formed, taking on the solid appearance of the men they once were.

'It's quite remarkable,' says Frederick Hardisty as he looks around. 'You, know, I can hardly believe they have built such a place.'

Is that not how it all started?

Boro managers since the club rose from the ashes of liquidation in 1986. Every single one of them can rightly claim to have taken the club forward...

'And such footballers,' replies Ossie Cochrane. 'Really, Fred, they quite put us to shame. They don't just boot the thing about, they're athletes...every one of them. Quite outstanding.'

'Such names too...' Mister Hardisty is almost laughing to himself. 'Pogatetz, Alves, Tuncay, Boateng, Rochembach, Schwarzer, Arca and Aliadiere. I hope I pronounce them properly...such talents.'

'And the other boys, Young and Riggott and the local lads, Downing, Wheater, Johnson…'

Mister Hardisty nods. 'I know that there'll be new names. There always are. Always someone to take the place of those who move on. But, even so…Mister Southgate and Mister Cooper, such clever men…it makes me so proud.'

'I think we all have good reason for pride, gentlemen.'

The two men look around to see who has just spoken as a flickering, semi-transparent form takes shape, pausing briefly to groom the enormous moustache that adorns his face.

'Mister Ewbank, I was wondering when you'd get here,' says Ossie Cochrane..

'Just been looking around. Have you seen the changing rooms? Bless me, we thought ourselves well served if there was a tree to shelter under. Well, well, what have we here?'

He looks down at the football.

'Are you thinking what I'm thinking?' wonders Frederick Hardisty.

'I don't see why not,' enthuse the others. 'After all it's a very poor show if you can't enjoy being young again, once you're dead!'

With that, Mister Cochrane takes a hefty swing at the ball with his boot and sends it arcing towards the centre circle.

Fred Hardisty is immediately after it, spinning on a sixpence to send it back towards Jackson Ewbank who, with one unerring kick, sends it between the goalposts. Ossie Cochrane chases and retrieves it, punts it upfield for the others to race after.

As the kickabout progresses, more and more translucent shapes emerge from the black shadows of the players' tunnel and take on form. All appear wearing a different style and variation of shirt, some of them are white, either plain or with the blue-and-white polka dots, some wear dark blue, but there is one colour that dominates, in a multitude of versions, with or without white collar and cuffs, or the white shoulders or the white chest band, all are unmistakeably blood-red.

The ball bobbles to a halt in front of Mister Hardisty as he observes the approaching throng.

'I think they want to join in,' says Jackson Ewbank.

'Well, there's not a man among them who hasn't earned the right,' says Mister Cochrane.

'But it won't work!' insists Mister Hardisty, laughing as he says it. 'We'll end up with over 40 or more on each side!'

Ossie Cochrane swings his leg and hits the ball high into the air while everyone scrambles immediately after it.

'Why not?' he grins. 'After all, isn't that how it all started?'